God's Fingerprint

God's Fingerprint

Principles for fruitful lives and churches

Paul Scanlon with Sue Smith

Hodder & Stoughton
LONDON SYDNEY AUCKLAND

First published in Great Britain in 1999

British Library Cataloguing in Publication Data
A record for this book is available from the British Library

ISBN 0 340 73538 4

Typeset by Avon Dataset Ltd, Bidford-on-Avon, Warks

Printed and bound in Great Britain by
The Guernsey Press Co. Ltd, Channel Isles

Hodder & Stoughton Ltd
A Division of Hodder Headline PLC
338 Euston Road
London NW1 3BH

I dedicate this book to my childhood sweetheart, now my wife of twenty-six years, Glenda. What can I say? You married me when I was sixteen and what a life we have had together so far. They say that behind every successful man there is a surprised woman, but that's not true of you. You have believed in me more than anyone I know. You are my best friend, I love you and I knew all along that one day I would make you famous.

Contents

Acknowledgements

Here is my salute to a few special people who have made this book possible.

To my writing partner, Sue Smith, who somehow managed to juggle the demands of a large family, church leadership and occasional e-mail failure. I salute you.

Charlotte Gambill, both my eldest daughter and my PA and secretary. You are far more than an employee; you are my right hand. Thanks for all the late nights of hard work. It has all been worthwhile and you can go home now.

Thanks to Stephen Matthew, my associate pastor, for all your editorial and proofreading skills.

Thank you to the Abundant Life Church family. I wrote about you all in Chapter 6 and I remembered everything you told me to say.

Thank you to the family at Hodder and Stoughton Publishers. Thanks for getting on board with us, taking a chance and publishing an unknown author.

My final salute goes to you, the reader. I am so aware that you are about to entrust me with your most precious gift, your time. Thank you, and may God enrich and refresh your life for doing so.

1

Growth – God's DNA

The two fields stretched away up the hillside, bathed in the evening sunlight. Couples strolled along hand in hand, villagers trudged home after a long day's work, travellers passed through, and all stopped to look at the scene before them. The two fields belonged to different owners; a fact that was as evident as if someone had put up a notice informing passers-by. One field was bursting with ripening crops, their golden tips rippling in perfect rows, the earth beneath them showing rich and dark, with no weeds to hide it. As people's gaze moved from this vista of pleasing order and fruitfulness, it came to rest on the adjacent field with an almost physical shock. No longer one of productivity and abundance, the picture was now one of chaos and hostility. Fierce thorn bushes thrust upwards, overwhelming shorter plants and suffocating them. Bindweed snaked through the stunted crops, strangling the life out of them. The plants that had managed to survive were pale and depleted, languishing in the shadow of the rampant weeds. Dark insects crawled everywhere, sucking the nutrients from the plants and leaving them ragged and brown. The ground was rocky and hard, littered with stones

1

from the crumbling boundary walls.

People shook their heads as they moved on down the road. 'I wouldn't like to harvest *that* field,' said one, pushing away an overhanging bramble. 'Who does it belong to?'

'Oh, that belongs to the village sluggard,' replied another. 'He put in some seed – borrowed, mind – at the beginning of spring, but he hasn't been back since. I reckon he's going to get a bit of a shock when he does! He certainly won't get anything good out of it.'

The village sluggard is mentioned frequently in the book of Proverbs, and his field is described in chapter 24 verses 30–34. His story highlights an important principle beyond the obvious one about the consequences of laziness. The principle is that growth is a fundamental element of creation. It is written into the natural and spiritual laws of existence. The lack of work on the sluggard's part did not prevent growth from happening. Although the *desired* crop was not present at harvest time, there had nonetheless been abundant growth during the months of neglect. A great deal had grown, none of which was useful and all of which would need to be pulled out before any more crops could be planted and nourished there.

So also, in our own lives and communities, *something* is always growing. Growth happens without reference to us, because it is obeying a law of nature over which we have no control. What grows might not be what we desire or intend, but it is nonetheless there. The aim of this book is to examine the various principles involved in growth, what aids it and what hinders it, how negative growth in one area of life inevitably affects all other areas, and to discover how we can utilise these principles in our personal lives and in our church communities. It is a book to encourage individuals and churches to realise their own potential for increase and fulfilment, and to take steps to enable it to happen.

We all need to grow. It's a basic human requirement, like food or sleep. As long as we live, we grow, physically, mentally and spiritually (even if it's only to grow old!). *What* and *how* we grow is the key issue and the main theme of this book. As children, our physical and mental growth is most evident, but it does not stop when we are adults. Our bodies are constantly replenishing their cells, with new ones growing to replace the old. Hair, nails, brain cells and skin: all are in a ceaseless process of growth. The same is true of our intellectual and emotional development. A quick review of how you were a few years ago compared to now will confirm this! We change and develop through experience, learning and, as Christians, by the power of the Holy Spirit. Also, all of us have 'seeds' in us. There is the physical seed, which may or may not produce another human, and there are 'idea seeds', dreams of what we would like to achieve, embryonic possibilities for the future, goals to achieve in both the natural and the spiritual realm. Some of these seeds come to fruition, while others wither away through neglect or lack of the right environment to thrive and prosper.

God desires positive, fruitful growth in people and in his church. He has immense plans for the world, and these can only happen as his people increase in their capacity. The Bible shows through teaching and role models that God's norm, both naturally and spiritually,

3

is to be successful and to reproduce. 'Success', of course, means different things to different people, but in this context it means to be productive, fulfilling God's potential at every level.

In Genesis 1, we find that productivity and fruitfulness were written into the very DNA of creation. Both naturally and spiritually, the law of reproduction is inherent in all of creation, including humanity. God's purpose in creating man was 'to make man in [his] image, in [his] likeness, and let them rule' (Genesis 1:26). The pinnacle of creation was to fill the earth with people like God. The driving force of our life is to be like him and to 'be fruitful and increase in number; fill the earth and subdue it' (Genesis 1:28). We cannot settle for anything less than that as the foundation of our experience. We are destined to grow and develop; it is as much part of our make-up as the breathing reflex.

Increase is a law of creation. The sluggard did nothing to tend his field and vineyard, yet he still had plenty growing. *Neglect, as much as diligence, will have a full garden,* because the law of increase operates regardless. Neglect, laziness and refusal to manage and be pro-active are not neutral things. Proverbs 24 tells us that the consequences of 'a little sleep, a little slumber' are not emptiness but the wrong kind of fullness. In other words, our abdication doesn't prevent growth, it simply and tragically allows the wrong kind of growth to develop. In failing to be pro-active in the management of growth, the sluggard of Proverbs 24 released the dual assault of the 'bandit of poverty' and the 'armed man of scarcity' into his field. These two robbers are active in the individual, the church and the nation, because those given the responsibility to manage busy themselves instead with distractions, putting off the priorities that growth demands. The point is that doing nothing always releases negative growth. Good things do not grow by themselves. They are the result of someone's deliberate and careful growth management. The issue then is not 'will the garden be full?' but 'what will it be full of?'

Deliberate growth

Unless we get very deliberate about growth, we will not grow in the way that we want to. The principles that govern natural growth can also be applied to spiritual development. I once watched a gardening programme on television where someone produced the most enormous carrot imaginable. It was a monster among carrots, and at first I thought it was a model. But no, it was a real vegetable, grown from the same seed as other, lesser carrots. The proud gardener who had produced this giant described how he had developed a conscious strategy to grow massive prize-winning carrots. He chose the finest seed, cleared ground, removing all hindrances to growth, and treated the soil months in advance of planting. Once the seed was planted, he fed it with all sorts of special products, so that it became a carrot of unusual dimensions. It was still a carrot, but as large and as perfect as possible. I believe that God wants both prize-winning lives and prize-winning churches, but in order to be that we must become deliberate about our growth.

We too can prepare the ground, feed the soil and nurture that which grows so that it is large and healthy. We want our productivity, whether in private, family or church life, to be of unusual dimensions. In order to reach the world, we need to be big. So often, we know what qualities we want to flourish, yet they become submerged or stunted by other, negative, weed-like characteristics that have developed with great vigour and eclipsed that which we would really like to see happen. Just as one might feel daunted by seeing a garden overtaken by weeds, so we can feel overwhelmed at the very thought of uprooting the undesirable in our lives or churches and clearing the ground for fruitful, godly growth. Yet it is vital that we do so, in order that there might be the kind of growth God requires.

Genesis 1 is the first time we see God's giving in action. He created and sowed only once. After that, everything else had to continue reproducing itself. He gave creation the power and commission to do so. God planted the world, and then the world continued to replant itself. *Everything God controls, gives.* Humans also were given the power and the inner motivation to reproduce themselves. In our lives and churches, we have to embrace this fundamental principle if we are to be fruitful and multiply.

The episode of the fig tree in Matthew 21 stands as a salutary warning to anyone who regards growth and productivity as an overrated emphasis. Why did Jesus react so strongly to the fig tree's failure to bear fruit? One might expect him to shrug his shoulders philosophically, encourage self-control in his disciples and set off speedily for food elsewhere. T. Austen Sparks, in his book *The*

Reality of the Cross of Christ (Barbour, 1987), sees the story as a 'parable of unfulfilled trust, receiving without passing on'. The tree was a living violation of its creational mandate, and so is much of the church. It took Jesus to see the invisible and expose it, leaving us in no doubt that God sees fruitfulness to be of the utmost importance.

As a man thinks

The greatest hindrance to growth is psychological. For this reason, we need to explore the law which states 'As a man thinks in his heart so is he' (Proverbs 23:7). In other words, we are what we think, not what we eat or do. How we think is the most powerful influence in our lives. Indeed, it is more powerful in its effect upon us than even how God thinks about us. The context of Proverbs 23:6–7 is very instructive. 'Do not eat the food of a stingy man, for as a man thinks in his heart so is he. Even though he says to you "eat and drink", his heart is not with you, he is always thinking about the cost and he begrudges you taking his food' (Proverbs 23:6–7, *Amplified Bible*, my paraphrase).

Here is a picture of a miserly man trying to appear generous but failing to sustain the masquerade because he can't stop thinking about the cost. And the reason for this? Because he is a stingy man in his heart. He is simply unable to be anything other than how he thinks. As a man thinks, as a church thinks, as a nation thinks, so they are – it's a law of life. Notice that it is 'as' or 'how' a man thinks, not 'what' a man thinks. What we think about any given subject is governed by the way in which we think about the bigger picture. So, for example, it is possible to have a generous thought while not thinking as a generous person. It is possible to have a big thought while not thinking big. *A big thought does not make you a big person*, any more than a bar of soap, a bath and a ribbon make a pig a poodle!

We are all pre-programmed

It is helpful to view this in computer terms. We are all pre-programmed. As you read this book, your inner software has already been programmed by a whole series of things going back as far as your childhood. It is amazing how certain ways of thinking can lie dormant for years until triggered by an attempt to think outside their permissions and boundaries. On a recent trip to Australia and New Zealand, my wife, Glenda, and I stood one day watching people bungee-jumping off a bridge into the oblivion below. I asked the lady selling the tickets (yes, people were actually paying to do this!) if she had ever bungee-jumped herself. 'Yes,' she replied, 'but when I first did it, I nearly backed out at the last minute.' She went on to explain that as she stood all roped up, her toes dangling over the abyss below, seconds before she jumped she suddenly heard the voice of her mother, who was long dead, shouting in her mind, 'Don't stand near the edge.' She froze and was about to turn back when she heard the crowd behind her shouting in unison, 'Five, four, three, two, one . . .' She was too embarrassed to turn around and refuse to jump and so,

ignoring her mother's voice – a strong software programming triggered by her act of violation – she leapt off
into mid-air. She was a 56-year-old grandmother, and that
day she broke an ancient barrier in her life. She had
jumped many times since, and apart from maybe being a
little taller, she not only had survived the jumps but was
now actively encouraging others to do the same. It is
amazing how certain parts of our programming can
remain inactive for years until aroused by some new
thought or behaviour threatening its control over our
lives.

We have always done it this way

The church is riddled with a 'we have always done it
this way' mentality, and it is killing us. If you were to ask
the question 'Why?' about procedures, routines or events
in your church, you would be amazed how often the
reply 'Because we have always done it this way' comes
back at you.

A young bride was preparing a ham shank roast for
her husband, and as she was about to cut off the end of
the ham joint, he interrupted by asking her a never-
before-asked question: 'Why do you always cut off the
end of the ham before putting it into the pan?'

'Because we have always done it this way.'

Her husband persisted. 'Yes, but why?'

Her reply confused him even further: 'Because my
mother taught me to do it that way.' He insisted that she
phone her mother with this unheard-of question.

'Mum, why did you teach me to cut off the end of the

ham whenever we had a ham shank roast at home?'

Her mother replied, 'I don't know, your grandmother taught me to do it.'

Fortunately, Grandma was still around to question. Her reply was, amazingly and simply, 'We always cut off the end of the ham because my pan was too small.'

And there you have it. For three generations, the end of the ham had been cut off simply because Grandma's pan was too small. It's a funny story, but absolutely tragic when the same is true in our lives and churches. I am constantly amazed at how many things are going on inside the church that have no more rhyme or reason to them than the above story. Growing lives and churches must not do things simply because 'we have always done it this way'. They cannot be wedded to ancient methods or old traditions, some of which have become 'sacred cows' – untouchable and unapproachable by any new thinking.

My mother-in-law, Betty Johnson, is a wonderful person. She is a sprightly and bright 76-year-old, but try as I might, I cannot get her to give up her twin-tub washer. On washday at her house, out comes the twin-tub to occupy the centre of her tiny kitchen. In no time at all, the place is transformed into a sauna, and Betty slogs it out, week in and week out, lifting washing from one tub to another and standing back hastily to take cover when the spin dryer kicks in. I have on several occasions tried to extol the virtues of an automatic washing machine to her, but to no avail.

'Oh, I've heard about those,' she says. 'They tear clothes, devour buttons, and leak.'

All is made clear when I realise that Mavis down the

road told her that. Mavis is her fellow twin-tub partner, and also in her seventies. Is there some kind of twin-tub enthusiasts' club that I don't know about in this country? What I do know, though, is that there is an awful lot of twin-tub Christianity about. People and leaders alike slogging it out, doing the same old things that don't work, while casting a suspicious and cynical eye over others doing things that do work and from whom they could learn so much. There can be fewer things more pointless than doing the same futile things year in, year out, yet expecting a different outcome, but people do this all the time.

Balls of new thought

Some of us have a little man sitting in our mind who acts like a Wimbledon line judge in the court of our thinking. He has been trained all his life to shout one word and one word only: 'OUT'. He never says 'in', only 'out'. Imagine if one day at a crucial point in a Centre Court match at Wimbledon, the line judge, upon realising that a ball he thought was going to be out was actually in, suddenly leapt to his feet and started shouting, 'In, in, in, the ball is in! Well done, that man! A few more shots like that and you will win the match!' It has never been seen or heard of, and never will be. Many people, and especially Christians, have a line judge sitting in their minds shouting 'out' every time a ball of new thought comes anywhere near the lines of permitted thought patterns he has drawn for them. Many calls of 'out' may have already been shouted in your mind as you began reading this book, so you must start overruling your line judge, because just one of those balls of new thought could be the very answer you have been waiting for.

Some people are so narrow-minded that that they can see through a keyhole with both eyes. They don't just have a line judge, they have Cyclops installed. Cyclops is the electronic eye that reads down the line and can tell more accurately than the human eye whether a ball is out or not. Often the line judge doesn't say 'out', but the machine emits its 'bleep bleep' sound, indicating an 'out' call. Recently at Wimbledon, an amazing thing happened. A tiny insect flew through the Cyclops beam and set it off. Cyclops bleeped 'out', but the ball wasn't even in play. Cyclops couldn't tell the difference between a fly and a ball, and neither can some people. It only takes a fly-sized new thought, never mind a ball-sized new thought, to completely throw some people, and even entire churches. Yet many of these people and churches are constantly crying out for more growth and breakthrough, never realising that the problem rests within the boundaries of their own limited thinking.

Some of us need to get a John McEnroe spirit. We need to run over to the line judge of our mind every time he shouts 'out' and get in his face with a loud, aggressive, 'You cannot be serious!!' It's worth fighting for every ball of new thought that is disputed, because just one new thought, idea or dream from God can change your life for ever. The good news is that the umpire is on your side. He's the Holy Spirit and loves to overrule the line judge, but he can't until you protest and contend for the point. The umpire of the Holy Spirit will back you up to the hilt. He wants to get in the line judge's face with you and shout, 'You cannot be serious! The ball is in, the ball was good, the point is given to my son, my daughter, my church.' We must rule the line judge in our mind by sending the signal that we will not just lie down and submit to his call. The apostle Paul (living before the days of tennis!) put it a different way in 2 Corinthians 10:4–5 when he said; 'For the weapons of our warfare are not carnal, but mighty through God to the pulling down of strong holds; Casting down imaginations, and every high thing that exalteth itself against the knowledge of God, and bringing into captivity every thought to the obedience of Christ' (King James Version).

Notice that, in Paul's terms, our weapons have divine power to demolish every argument from the small-minded controlling voices that seek to contain our lives. Divine power is the greatest power in the universe. It is greater than nuclear power. *Nuclear power isn't strong enough to change your mind, but divine power can change your life for ever*. Also note the word 'stronghold'. A stronghold is a fortress, a fortified walled structure to keep out any unwelcome visitors. Strongholds aren't built all at once. They are the end result of a process which, if unchallenged, will become a stronghold. *A stronghold starts at the threshold and if unchallenged becomes a foothold, then a stranglehold, and finally a stronghold*. It's time for every stronghold of the mind to come tumbling down, and I pray that this book will inspire you to assault some of your inner fortresses and break out into whole new ways of thinking.

Death by containment

There is such truth in the assertion I once heard that 'the devil isn't half as concerned about pushing you back as he is about containing you where you are'. Containment is just as effective as backsliding as an obstacle to growth. Many Christians who haven't openly given up on God, who still attend church meetings, still give financially, still serve and are even in leadership, are actually living contained lives. Containment means to be hemmed in, enclosed, restrained and confined. The problem with containment, however, is that most of us don't even realise it's going on. You may be reading this book in a room where the walls are containing you. Yet you don't feel contained, because you still have room to move and walk around. The problem occurs when we think that the limited amount of room we have to walk around in is our whole life. Sadly, many have settled for this, never knowing that they are actually being contained within the four walls of limitation and confinement that an enemy has slowly erected around their life.

The difficulty is that many people prefer to be contained. Sometimes, we are like people who reoffend just so that they can be sent back to prison. They prefer the safe predictability of a rigidly structured prison regime rather than the overwhelming freedom of being on the outside of those prison walls. *The simple truth is that it takes courage to live free*. Many people keep doing the same thing, staying inside the same comfort zones, the same relationships and the same safe decisions and routines. In this book I want to challenge you to break out of your containment and begin living freely, more freely than you ever thought possible. Growth requires freedom. A contained plant will eventually die if it is not repotted, and so will we. God wants to repot you into the vastness of your destiny, where there is room enough for a lifetime's growth without ever reaching the boundaries.

The Truman Show

A film I saw recently really brought this issue of containment home to me in a powerful way. It was called *The Truman Show*, and starred Jim Carey. The basic story was about a man who, as an orphaned baby, was given the name Truman and chosen to be filmed for the rest of his life, twenty-four hours a day. Unknown to him, his whole life was being broadcast on television all around the world, just as it happened, with no editing or adjustment. Truman was raised in a small town on the coast, never knowing that every person in that town was an actor, including his invented father, work colleagues and even his own wife. The town was covered by thousands of concealed TV cameras, some in his car and home, so tiny that they couldn't be detected. One day Truman, by now in his early thirties, received a tip-off from a young woman in the town library, who couldn't bear the facade of unreality any more.

The next day, now alerted to things not being as they seemed, Truman decided to do a number of spontaneous things he had never done before, just to see if he could detect anything to confirm his suspicions. He followed his wife, who was supposed to be a nurse, to work, only to be thrown out of the hospital by security men, who were, of course, actors. Crossing the street from the hospital, he ran into a hotel lobby where, behind the elevator doors, he glimpsed a film set with lights and technicians. Behind the scenes, the programme controllers were frantically trying to stay a step ahead of him, not knowing what he would do next. Truman had seen enough, and that night he slipped the cameras, stole a boat and set out to sea in an attempt to escape this strange world. Truman had an awful fear of water because his invented father had died an invented death by drowning, years earlier. Eventually, the programme producers found him and, because they also controlled the weather, sent a storm to force him to turn back again. The whole drama was being played out in front of viewers across the world. After almost drowning, he persisted and sailed on towards the horizon.

The film ends with an amazing scene I will never forget. As Truman sailed towards the horizon, not knowing how far he would have to go to reach land, his boat suddenly came to an abrupt halt. He looked in amazement towards the prow and saw that he couldn't go any further because the boat had bumped into a huge wall with sky painted on it. It was only then that he realised his whole life had been lived inside a huge dome. The town was inside the dome, and even the man-made ocean was inside it. As his boat hit the side of the dome, the Holy Spirit spoke to me and said, 'He has reached the limit of his containment, and now it's decision time.'

The film closes with Truman climbing a hidden stairway painted into the sky background and opening a concealed door at the top of these stairs. He hesitates as the voice of the programme controller comes booming from the sky inside the dome, appealing to him to turn around and come back, because all his life has been lived inside this contained world and beyond that door is the great unknown. The watching world holds its breath as he hesitates on the threshold of freedom. Truman slowly turns around and, taking a bow to the world he now realises is watching him, leaves his containment. The global audience breaks into applause as he finally escapes his contained life.

Some of you are living *The Truman Show*. You think you're free, but actually you are being contained by many things that are conspiring to keep your life smaller than God ever intended it to be. You have contained joy, contained faith, contained hope, contained peace, contained provision, contained health, contained success, contained thinking. You open your Bible and read about 'joy unspeakable and full of glory', and the words are meaningless to you. Or you read about 'the peace that passes understanding' and think to yourself, 'I don't know what that is.' You read about provision that's 'pressed down, shaken together and running over', and, confused, think, 'What in the world can that be?' I'll tell you what it is – your life! It's life beyond the wall of containment. It's your life and your church's life. Your life is not *The Truman Show*, it's 'The Truth Shall Set You Free Show'. It's necessary to get up and grab your life, break out of your containment and live it, love it and be as free as God meant you to be.

Some of you have been so contained that you never

did go for that career that you wanted. You never took that opportunity that came once in a lifetime. You never learnt to drive. You never learnt that language. You never said what you wanted to say, went where you wanted to go or bought what you wanted to buy. The good news, though, is that you can forget regret, for it's never too late to break out of your containment. Some people need to begin by doing small, seemingly irrelevant things which will help break patterns of containment, such as driving home a different way, getting a new hair-do, changing the wallpaper, buying something you don't need, eating something you've never tried, saying something that you know will get you into trouble when you always play it safe. Try barbecuing in winter, walking backwards for a day, bursting into song on the bus or in the dentist's waiting room! All these things will register the clear message with your soul: 'I will not live a contained life.' I see so many Christians who seem to have the name 'Gulliver' written over their head. God's word to them and to you is to leave Lilliput, leave the dome, break out of containment and go and live your life to the full; life as God truly intended it to be.

We must settle the issue that growth is normal and abandon our theologies (or should I say excuses?) for smallness. We should be just as concerned about the contained, stunted growth of a church as we would be if it were our own child in the natural. The human body has certain growth hormones, and a deficiency here can suppress normal growth. It's the same in the body of Christ; if we have a dysfunctional growth hormone – and many churches do – then the growth of the church will be just as stunted.

Let me clarify a few things from the outset. Some readers may already be thinking, 'Oh no, not another church growth book from an American theorist who has never led a church.' I am British, and have been in the same church for twenty-five years. I have been leading the church for fifteen years, and I'm as 'hands-on' and involved with every issue of church life as anyone reading this book.

Our growing church in the north of England is in the heart of Yorkshire, perhaps one of the most parochially minded counties in the nation. So if these principles of growth can work here, they can surely work anywhere. I have tried to avoid theories in this book, and instead share with you principles which we are practising. I believe a principle is worth a thousand methods. I have included as many personal and church examples as I have felt necessary to help illustrate and emphasise the principles. I am by no means an expert on these matters, but rather a fellow traveller trying to pass on some things that I would have really appreciated someone passing on to me in years gone by. I encourage you to grasp anything which is of use for the present and put the rest on a back burner for now.

If you can move forward into the remainder of this book with the kind of openness of mind and heart here described, then I believe you are on course for some breakthrough thinking. Why not pause here for a moment? Ask the Holy Spirit to help you to open your mind, so that you don't miss anything that he wants you to receive in order to achieve your maximum productivity.

Key Points

- Neglect, as much as diligence, will have a full garden.

- Everything God controls, gives.

- A big thought does not make you a big person.

- Nuclear power isn't strong enough to change your mind, but divine power can change your life for ever.

- A stronghold starts at the threshold and then if unchallenged becomes a foothold, then a stranglehold, and finally a stronghold.

- The simple truth is that it takes courage to live free.

2

Framing your world

The growth we seek needs to be securely established, otherwise it will founder. Just as a plant needs to be firmly rooted in the earth, drawing its nutrients from the soil beneath, so any growth we desire needs to be sustained from within ourselves. It is vital, therefore, that our inner selves are strong enough to support and cope with the demands of enlargement. Modern houses have a strong internal frame upon which the rest of the building is hung. Without it, the house would collapse under its own weight. Similarly, we choose the frame of our lives, and so dictate the amount of growth possible.

Big guns, small life

God wants us to have an inner life which is strong enough to sustain our outer one. Our inner life is the foundational anchor of all the growth that will ever take place through us. I remember this truth coming home so clearly to me many years ago as I sat looking out across San Diego harbour. I was looking at the huge navy destroyers and particularly at the powerful shell-firing guns mounted around the ships. Then, by contrast, I saw the tiny pleasure boats, bouncing along across the harbour. I began thinking about what would happen if one of those huge guns were to be mounted on the side of one of these little boats. The recoil action alone, which follows a shell being fired, would shatter one of these boats to pieces. Yet when the battleship fires the guns, even repeatedly, there is no visible sign of recoil impact on either the ship's structure or the water. These ships have been specially built and lined, with thick, solid steel hull and decks, to absorb the recoil without any disturbance or damage to the infrastructure.

Many people want to fire God's big guns, want big callings, big giftings and high-profile ministries, yet their lives have insufficient character lining to be able to handle the inevitable recoil. Many have been destroyed through the recoil of pressure, praise and opportunity which comes from doing great things for God in any high-profile way. *The simple truth is that the miracles through us must never be greater than the miracle in us.* Growth begins and is rooted in our secret life with God, and if it isn't then it won't last. If it *is* nourished and sustained from our inner world, then the growth will be abundant and fruitful. The writer of Proverbs points out that 'All a man's ways seem right to him, but the LORD weighs the heart' (Proverbs 21:2), and that 'As water reflects a face, so a man's heart reflects the man' (Proverbs 27:19). David, who himself cried out to God, 'Create in me a pure heart, O God, and renew a steadfast spirit within me' (Psalm 51:10), said of an erstwhile friend, 'His speech is smooth as butter, yet war is in his heart' (Psalm

55:21). I am sure that we have all met people with such paradoxical gaps in their make-up.

Sinkholes

In some people, this gap widens until it is unsustainable and collapse occurs. Gordon MacDonald, in his book *Ordering Your Private World*, calls it the 'sinkhole syndrome' and likens it to a phenomenon he saw in Florida, where underground subsidence had been occurring in a street for some time without anyone being aware of it. One morning, residents awoke to the sight of a massive hole outside their homes, into which pavements, lampposts, vehicles and garden furniture were all falling. It was evident that apartment blocks would soon follow. In the end, the subsidence had made itself known in a very destructive manner. MacDonald notes:

> The Florida sinkhole is a physical picture of a spiritual problem with which many Western Christians must deal. As the pressure of life grows ... there will be more people whose lives resemble a sinkhole, unless they gaze inwards and ask themselves, Is there a private world beneath the noise and action at the surface? A world that needs to be explored and maintained. Can strength and resilience be developed that will bear up under the pressure at the surface?
>
> (*Ordering Your Private World*, Gordon MacDonald, Highland Books, 1987)

A collapse from within can have tragic results – the breakdown of a marriage, family disruption, loss of a job, loss of health, loss of faith. These are extreme examples, but the danger is always there if we allow an element of unreality to exist in our lives.

Jesus develops this theme extensively in his teaching, highlighting the importance he gives to a person's internal life. In Matthew 5, he makes the radical statement that if a man even thinks lustful thoughts, he has committed adultery, and if he harbours anger in his heart, then he is 'subject to judgment' as much as if he had murdered. These are challenging words that would revolutionise our lives if we really took them seriously. But, too often, we allow much lower standards to operate in our private worlds than in our public ones. Yet we should heed the warnings:

> The word of God is living and active. Sharper than any double-edged sword, it penetrates even to dividing soul and spirit, joints and marrow; it judges the thoughts and attitudes of the heart. Nothing in all creation is hidden from God's sight. Everything is uncovered and laid bare before the eyes of him to whom we must give account.
>
> (Hebrews 4:12–13)

Whatever is growing within us will eventually come out. Jesus continues the natural metaphor when he also makes this point, likening people's lives to fruit-bearing trees:

> No good tree bears bad fruit, nor does a bad tree bear

good fruit. Each tree is recognised by its own fruit. People do not pick figs from thorn-bushes, or grapes from briers. The good man brings good things out of the good stored up in his heart, and the evil man brings evil things out of the evil stored up in his heart.

(Luke 6:43–5)

So, for fruitful, positive growth to occur in our lives, our families, our churches and our nation, it has to start in each individual's inner, intimate world. We might try to prosper in external things, but it is futile unless our internal lives are thriving as well. A family may appear to be united and do all sorts of things together, but if the relationships within it are sour or distant then it is not prospering in the areas that really matter. The church might attempt a programme of events to encourage fellowship evangelism and various other initiatives, but if the core life of the church – that is, each individual's relationship with God – is not thriving, then the most ambitious of programmes will ultimately flounder.

All visible things have invisible beginnings

One of the principles I will develop in this book is that all growth begins invisibly. We find this creational principle in Hebrews 11:3. 'By faith we understand that the universe was formed at God's command, so that what is seen was not made out of what was visible.' In other words, God's invisible words of command created a visible universe. *All visible things have invisible beginnings*. Great inventions begin as invisible ideas in someone's mind, and can remain that way for long periods before they actually take on a tangible shape. Organisations and movements begin with invisible words and concepts and grow to be large, successful business empires. All of what grows and develops in our lives begins in the invisible realm; words, thoughts, ideas and dreams – all, gradually or swiftly, take on a visible form. Your career, house, friendships, hobbies and even your car all began with invisible desires, thoughts and imaginings. What we must understand is that, though these things are invisible, they are no less real than when they later develop into something visible and tangible. Is a woman pregnant before she knows she is pregnant? Of course she is. Though its beginnings are hidden, secret and unfelt, the baby is just as real as it will ever be.

Words are seeds

Your words are seeds. Jesus states this when he tells the parable of the sower in Matthew 13. When he explains the parable, he says the seed is 'the message about the kingdom'. When someone is born again, an 'incorruptible seed' is planted in his life – the message that he believed and accepted. This then produces a tangible result as the life of Christ changes his actions and lifestyle. Other seeds do not always have such a beneficial result. If there are negative thought and behaviour patterns in your life, if it seems dogged by problems and depression, look for the invisible seed – those words, maybe recently, maybe in the past, which were scattered over you, settled in you and took root.

Once, when I was buying some perfume for my wife, the lady at the cosmetics counter said to me, 'Sir, let me show you the best way to wear perfume.' She sprayed Chanel No 5 into the air in front of her and then walked into it. As I watched the demonstration closely enough so that I could show this brilliant technique to my wife later on, the Holy Spirit said to me, 'Your words are like that.' Every time you open your mouth, you spray invisible words into the air and then you walk into them. Many people who are wearing their own negative confession are going around saying, 'I wonder where all this negative stuff came from in my life.' Some of us simply need to change what we are spraying and thereby change what we and others around us are walking into. If you spray it, you will wear it, so ensure that the perfume is right.

If we do not understand the principle of the visible being rooted in the invisible, then we are in danger of being robbed by an enemy who does understand the principle. In Jesus' parable, birds, thistles and stones did their best to stop the invisible word seed from taking root. The enemy will always be more active at planting than he will at harvest, because he knows that it's the invisible beginnings that are the most crucial to the growth of the crop. If something is wrong in the invisible realm, you can't correct it by dealing with the visible signs. That would be like slashing at overgrown foliage to get rid of it, but leaving the root. Before long, the weeds would return, even more ferociously! It's imperative to go back to the source. The external problems are only a symptom of something unseen that needs changing.

Fairy rings

When we first moved into our present house, we noticed that there were some strange dark rings on the lawn. I wondered if they were oil marks from a mower, but closer inspection revealed that the grass was dying, yet only in these small circles. More experienced gardeners told us, with a despondent shake of the head, that these were known as 'fairy rings'. For the first year, we just kept feeding and mowing the lawn, hoping that tender loving care and a good diet would do the trick. But it didn't. The rings were still there and seemed to be spreading. We consulted experts, who said that the only way to stop them was to dig down a foot deep and two foot wide across the lawn to get rid of the contaminated soil. It was discovered that when the lawn was first laid, the builders had left old, rotten wood in the soil underneath the turf. This rotting timber had released spores into the earth which then grew, infected the grass and created the fairy rings. Treating the surface of the lawn, or even the topsoil, was not enough; completely new soil had to be put in after the old had been dug up and taken away.

Often, we need to do the same with the fairy rings in our lives. It is no good dealing with the symptoms of the trouble, whether it be wrong behaviour patterns, loss of sleep, headaches, arguments or any other nagging problem. We need to dig down to the invisible root – perhaps an adverse reaction to something said to us, perhaps a fear of being hurt, perhaps an inner belief that we are not good enough. These need to be removed, maybe with the help of 'experts', certainly with the help of the Holy

Spirit, and then new seed planted, based on the word of God.

God framed the universe with invisible words (Hebrews 11:3), and we also frame our world with our own invisible words, invisible thoughts and attitudes. It is similar to the house-building technique where a wooden shell is put up first, and then everything is built up round it. Everyone has a world-framing faith. The world you inhabit might not be the one you desire, but it is nonetheless the one you have formed with the words, expectations and convictions within you. The good news is that it is possible to reframe the world you want to live in by going to the invisible realm and scattering or spraying some different seeds at the source. Eventually, that new, unseen seed will produce a discernible crop in your life.

Many people live in the thrall of past experiences which have damaged them and which have changed them over the years. Certainly, no one would deny the harm that comes from cruelty, abuse and neglect, nor wish to withdraw compassion and understanding from those who have suffered. But there comes a point when we *choose* whether we let those experiences frame our life or not, We do not have to be ruled by the negative; we can make a positive decision to allow other, better seed to grow, seed that comes straight from the Creator. *If we do not get assertive about framing our life, something or someone else will do it for us*. How sad it would be to look back in old age and realise that our life was never really as we wanted it, but always subject to the framing words or dictates of someone else, such as parents, boss, friends or culture.

The good news, however, is that it is possible to frame the kind of life we desire by starting in the invisible realm, speaking and thinking in a way which triggers into the visible world that which we want for our lives. This is not the power of positive thinking, but co-operating with the word of God and his principles of increase. We need to be diligent in framing our lives and operating the rule of the invisible and visible; then we will have the kind of bumper harvest we desire. If life seems to be full of thorns, weeds and thistles at present, don't keep fighting them back, but dig down to the roots, find out where the seed is coming from and change it. Weed-fighting people get worn out battling with the symptoms instead of changing the seed and awaiting a new crop. The problem is not the weeds – it's the seeds.

The power of the tongue

The tongue can get us all into trouble, and there are times for all of us when we bitterly regret the things we have said. Once the words are out, it is very difficult to put right any damage done. We all possess this boneless creature, deadlier than any serpent, lurking behind the enamel fence at the front of our mouth – the tongue. It strikes quicker than lightning. It can kill, destroy and damage without mercy. It could be said to have destroyed more lives than any weapon of modern warfare.

There was once a man who, as he became older, realised that he had done a lot of damage in his community by speaking badly about people, stirring up trouble, not dealing with conflict properly, but defaming his opponents instead. As time went by, he was increasingly conscience-stricken about the harm that he had done. So he went to the local priest and confessed his sins. He wanted to put things right with the people he had hurt. The priest told him to go round the town that night and put a bag of feathers on the doorstep of every person he had wronged. Perplexed at such a strange request but willing to do any penance which might ease his conscience, the man did as he was told and then reported to the priest. He was told to return to the town the next night and pick up all the feathers again. Much later that night, the man arrived at the priest's house in a distraught state. All the feathers had gone, scattered throughout the town, settling imperceptibly in all sorts of unexpected places. It was impossible for him to get them back. 'And so it is,' said the priest, 'with your words. Once they're spoken you can't get them back. They're all over the place, either blessing people or hurting them.'

Such is the power of that small member of the body. The tongue is so forceful and powerful that we must learn how to bridle it. The Bible consistently confirms this: 'Life and death are in the power of the tongue' (Proverbs 18:21). Everything we say is one or the other. There is nothing in between. Christians need to model a life-giving mode of speech, spreading positive, honourable, praiseworthy seeds whenever we speak.

It must have been a fool who said, 'Sticks and stones will break my bones but words can never hurt me,' because it just isn't true. Words hurt. Friendships, families, marriages, churches have been wrecked by the power of poisoned words. Some people are still hurting from things said many years ago. The words spoken to them so damaged them that, though they've gone forward in life, they have carried the wounds inside. God's advice is 'get over it and move on'. He offers comfort and healing, and encouragement to keep taking a step at a time until you are free from the issues which cause such pain. Don't let your life be held to ransom by words; you are far too valuable to let that happen.

In Proverbs 6:16, the writer speaks of seven things which God hates. Three of them are concerned with the tongue: a lying tongue, a false witness and a sower of discord. Jesus warns that 'men will have to give account on the day of judgment for every careless word they have spoken' (Matthew 12:36). Such a sobering prospect should encourage us to follow David's example and state, 'I will keep my tongue with a bridle' (Psalm 39:1, King James Version). A bridle is quite repressive, an instrument of force to achieve compliance from the horse. Sometimes we drop the reins and our mouth takes off, leaving in its wake a trail of damage and devastation. David understood the value of the bridle, and knew that he needed to exert such control on his own tongue.

Excuses such as 'I said it without thinking' do not stand up under scrutiny. If we couldn't help what we said, then it would be unjust of God to judge us for every careless word that we speak. Many parts of the body, such as the heart and the breathing and digestive systems, operate without our conscious control, but everything else requires thought and decision. Your tongue cannot operate without permission from you, for it has no involuntary movement. We can choose to control what we say, and this comes most easily when we have only good things growing within. Then, 'out of the overflow of [our] heart, [our] mouth speaks'.

Happiness is an inside job!

Happiness springs from within our private world. Many people who claim to have true freedom are deeply unhappy, because true freedom is not the right to do what we want but the power to live as we should, and only God knows how that should be. The only influence we should be under is God's. Everyone's desire, however disguised it may be, is to live in peace on the inside, wholesome in mind, emotions and intellect. To achieve such a desire, we have to understand that what is governing us is not external circumstances but our inner response to those circumstances.

So many people don't realise this and focus on all sorts of externals in an effort to be happy: more money, marriage, babies, status, a different age or stage in life, a job, retirement. They think that they will feel better on the inside by acquiring all that they want in life. But, so often, expectations do not match reality, and in striving for these things they miss the values which are really important, such as relationships with partner and children, friendships, loyalty and honour. *Happiness is not your position, it's your disposition*. The apostle Paul was happier in prison, wounded from flogging, chained up and singing to God, than many people today in easy conditions. No one can take away your freedom to choose your attitude.

In his teaching on the Mount of Olives, Jesus gave

some keys to true happiness: a string of seven pearls of priceless wisdom for a prosperous life, otherwise known as the Beatitudes (Matthew 5, *Message* Version). You will be truly happy and at peace (blessed) when:

- You're at the end of your rope; there's less of you and more of God (the poor in spirit).
- You feel you've lost that which is most dear to you; only then can you be embraced by the One most dear to you (those who mourn).
- You're content with just who you are – no more, no less; that's when you find yourself proud owners of everything that cannot be bought (the meek).
- You've worked up a good appetite for God. He's food and drink in the best meal you'll ever eat (hunger and thirst after righteousness).
- You care. At the moment of being care-full, you find yourself being cared for (the merciful).
- You get your inside world – mind and heart – put right. Then you can see God in the outside world properly (the pure in heart).
- You can show people how to co-operate instead of compete and fight. That's when you discover who you really are and your place in God's family (the peacemakers).

This is God's prescription for happiness in the human experience, and, if applied seriously, it is revolutionary in its effect. It is all summed up in Christ. To know him is to step into the source of true happiness and joy.

Self-control

Mankind has now learnt how to control many elements that were formerly beyond our power: solar heat, river forces, satellites, diseases, to name but a few. The pace of development in this century has been increasingly rapid. Yet in all of this amazing progress, self-control – the ability to do what you should, when you should, and not to do what you shouldn't – seems to have eluded the human race. Without self-control, we will all self-destruct, no matter who we are or what power or possessions we have. Every day, we see in the newspapers or on the television people who live the dream of most ordinary folk, and yet do not have the self-control to cope with it. The sad stories of seemingly successful politicians, footballers, film stars or businessmen whose inner lives are a disaster are paraded regularly to titillate a public who also struggle to achieve self-control. Even the most powerful man in the world, responsible for the lives and well-being of millions of people, chose not to deny himself the excitement of sordid extramarital sexual entertainment. A talented footballer missed the ultimate tournament because he had indulged in so much drink and self-abuse that he couldn't play properly any more. So many people ruin their own dreams because they refuse to control their inner desires and appetites. The sinkhole within them collapses, causing untold damage. And Christians are not immune from this problem either. Many 'great' men of God, famous for their preaching, books or television appearances, have discovered that their inner, private life was way behind their public projection of themselves, and eventually they could not disguise the ever-widening chasm. *It is vital that we all cultivate our inward garden and frame our inner world so that we have Christ's life in every area.*

The book of Proverbs points out how important the ability to discipline oneself is: 'Like a city whose walls are broken down is a man who lacks self-control' (Proverbs 25:28). The city of York provides a graphic illustration of this proverb. The walls still encircle most of the city and are high and strong, towering above the roads and unassailable. They can be entered only through fortified entrances which at one time had portcullises. But there are some places where the walls have broken down and disappeared, and people can freely walk into the city wherever they want. In former, more warlike times, such a breach in the walls would have serious consequences, making the city vulnerable to attack and invasion. This is what the Lord likens to someone who loses self-control. That person is vulnerable to being taken over by all sorts of hostile forces. If people truly practised self-control, our prisons would empty and our crime rate would decrease dramatically, marriages would remain strong, and children would grow up healthy and secure. It is not enough to say 'I can't help it', for God has given us a spirit of self-control (2 Timothy 1:7) to enable us to control our own inner desires. It may not be easy, but it is not impossible.

The greatest battles we will ever face are battles within ourselves. James, writing to the church, rebukes them for arguing and points out that the problem actually lies within the individuals, rather than in external causes. 'What causes fights and quarrels among you? Don't they come from your desires that battle within you?' (James 4:1). If you can master your attitudes, moods, thinking, emotions, then the external circumstances will not be such a threat.

Manage your moods

Christians are some of the moodiest people I have ever met, and moodiness betrays a failure to frame rightly our inner world. To be moody means to be changeable, fickle, temperamental, volatile, depressive. A moody person has good days and bad days, is sometimes 'not quite himself', is friendliness personified one minute and frosty the next, dominated by feelings and often in a dark place of heaviness. *We must manage our moods or our moods will manage us*.

I once went to sunny California, and was astonished on arrival to see that it was raining. When I arrived at the church building where I was to speak, the steward, knowing I was from England, said jokingly, 'Did you bring this weather with you?' The truth is, though, that we all bring weather with us. Our mood will dispense sunshine, gloom, frost or too much heat. We can choose every morning what kind of weather we will bring with us to family, workplace, school, church or friends' homes. We do not have to allow our moods to rule us, but with God's help we can get them under control. Here are a few helpful steps in managing moods.

Decide to manage your moods Make a decision, a commitment to it. That decision is refusing to accept that moods are beyond control. The moment you believe that your moods are not controllable then you've lost the battle. You do not have to live under the dark dominant moods you have lived under, for you are more powerful than your moods. Atrocious circumstances do not have to determine the inner man. The 'Spirit of self-control' was given as a gift by the Holy Spirit, which means we can control our thinking, moods and feelings.

Open up, don't blow up Many people come home from work full of repressed frustrations and take it out on the family. The atmosphere in the home becomes oppressive. Try to open up before you blow up. Spend time with a friend and talk about the things which are affecting you, the frustration and anger of work. Break the pattern and become more positive.

Identify patterns If you can't see it, ask someone who can. What is causing the pattern? Why do you feel in this mood at these times? Most people just wait until the mood passes, without dealing with its root. If we can try to express how we feel and can identify causes and patterns, then we can break the pattern. Ascertain whether you are under another influence than God's. Some people believe that they are under the influence of the past, that their moods are inherited, or caused by a bad childhood, or in the genetic makeup. Identify that belief and then dismantle it. Some people are taking mood-altering medications. Know what you are taking, and ask your GP if there is an alternative. Determine only to live under the influence of positive things in your life. Discern the seasons of the soul. You will not be on permanent spring, and that's fine. There will be times when you feel emotionally drained and spent. It's important not to make major decisions and commitments at those times. Jesus often withdrew to solitary places when he realised he was getting exhausted emotionally and needed to recharge his batteries.

Accept full responsibility Stop blaming things, events or people for them. 'Do not be deceived: God cannot be mocked. A man reaps what he sows' (Galatians 6:7). If it's there, it's there because it's been sown. If you're reaping it, you've allowed it to grow inside your life, but it can equally be removed and replaced by something else.

Adjust your 'thinking dial' Don't tune in to unhelpful signals. 'Whatever is true, whatever is noble, whatever is right, whatever is pure, whatever is lovely, whatever is admirable – if anything is excellent or praiseworthy – think about such things' (Philippians 4:8). If what you are thinking about doesn't fit any of those categories, turn the dial.

Keep your chin up Your body can affect your mind in the same way that your mind can affect your body. If your physical posture lines up with what you think and what you feel, you are entertaining the thoughts with your body as well as your mind, confirming them and allowing them more room. If you feel depressed, get up and stand straight, go for a brisk walk, talk to a positive friend. The phrase 'keep your chin up' has a lot of truth in it! If you can stop your body sliding into the mood as well, then there is more chance of controlling the mood.

Reprogramme your memory bank Moods are determined primarily by a combination of past experiences and expectations of future experiences. Life begins with a dot on a blank screen and is recorded from the womb onwards. Much we forget, but some lingers to do damage. We try to repress the bad recordings, but they emerge as a bad mood or negative emotion. The only way to heal and wipe out the past is to allow Christ to operate on us and reprogramme some of the recordings.

Start early

Self-control begins in childhood. The out-of-control five-year-old becomes the out-of-control fifteen-year-old who becomes an out-of-control adult, unable to conduct relationships properly, damaging those around him. It is important that parents discipline their children, so that they then learn self-discipline. If a child has never known any consistent control, how can he know how to control himself? Setting boundaries, consistent firmness, loving punishment when they transgress, encouragement in the work ethic, will all teach the child how to deal with his own inner emotions and impulses.

So many factors can cause us to go out of control. Temper, perhaps. 'A quick-tempered man does foolish things' (Proverbs 14:17). Loss of temper can ruin family life, damage friendships, induce headaches or other stress-related illnesses. Anger itself is not wrong, but the way we handle it often is. Or maybe our lack of control lies in a desire to spend. We find ourselves spending lots of money to buy things we don't even need, often to impress people we don't even like. Debts run up before we know it, and we are in a financial hole that seems impossible to climb out of.

Others cannot control their eating. The craving to eat and its converse, the need to lose weight, dominate their lives, creating a vicious circle of misery and low self-esteem. Or perhaps alcohol is the problem. It started as social drinking, but now has become a necessity to combat the stresses of life. For many others, the sexual drive is out of control. God's instruction to remain celibate until marriage and then not to have any other sexual partner seems too harsh in the light of racing hormones and an immoral culture. Yet the deadly pay-off of emotional, physical and mental damage in an ever-widening ripple effect speaks for itself. Peptic ulcers, heart problems, stress, insomnia, hypertension and AIDS can all be traced back in a large degree to a failure to control oneself.

God does not want this way of life for anyone. He lists self-control as one of the fruits of the Spirit (Galatians 5:23), contrasting it with the 'acts of the sinful nature' and pointing out that such acts were crucified with Christ. They no longer wield any power. And that is the key to managing our inner life and ensuring that we are whole people, the same in private as in public, not living even the smallest lie. We do not have to achieve this in our own strength. God does require that we turn from those things which we know are wrong, but he gives us the power to do it. Our deepest, most intimate place, where we are truly ourselves, is inhabited by the Holy Spirit. Once we have a continuing awareness of that amazing fact, we will be transformed by the authority and love which is actually within us. With the ground cleared of all impediments, it is easy for the growth of wholesome, enriching characteristics to take place. Our inner life will be abundant, fulfilling and productive, creating new seed which will affect other lives besides our own. And so God's creational law of increase continues, beginning in the individual life and multiplying outwards and onwards.

Key Points

- The simple truth is that the miracles through us must never be greater than the miracles in us.

- All visible things have invisible beginnings.

- If we do not get assertive about framing our life, something or someone else will do it for us.

- Happiness is not your position, it's your disposition.

- It is vital that we cultivate our garden and frame our inner world so that we have Christ's life in every area.

- We must manage our moods or our moods will manage us.

3

How to stay strong when it all goes wrong

The waves crashed across the bow of the boat, filling the bottom and soaking the men as they desperately struggled to tether the sails and row for the shore. The small vessel tackled each ceaseless, towering mountain of water, rearing up and then lurching down, all the time taking on more water. The fierce wind, roaring its fury, constantly knocked the boat off course, nearly causing it to keel over. The men, their voices sharpened by fear, yelled commands and counter-commands at each other, straining to keep the boat upright and afloat.

In the stern, a man lay sleeping on a cushion, oblivious to the spectacular storm and the danger of the situation. The exhausted sailors, almost on the point of giving up, ran and shook him awake, hardly able to believe that he was still asleep in such conditions. 'Teacher! Teacher! Wake up! We're going to drown! Don't you care that we're in such danger?'

He looked at them, taking in much more than the immediate circumstances, then got up and addressed the raging elements, while his friends stared in bewilderment.

43

'Quiet! Be still!' Jesus shouted. The silence was immediate and uncanny. The fermenting, turbulent sea turned into a peaceful millpond and the thunderous wind was no longer even a whisper of breeze. Jesus smiled at the shaken sailors, as if he had done nothing unusual. 'Why were you so frightened?' he asked. 'Do you still have no faith?' Not knowing what to say, they returned to their tasks, discussing the whole amazing event among themselves as they went. The disciples were on a steep learning curve.

Many people and churches give up on growth because they get overwhelmed by the demands it brings and the things that can go wrong along the way. They begin to question whether growth is worth all the effort and start to sink into unbelief and doubt. Then the kind of containment which I spoke about in Chapter 1 begins to creep in. Everything that grows must face resistance at some point, and what I want to show you in this chapter is the importance of staying strong when everything seems to be going wrong.

Sometimes, even when we have done our best to follow after God and be obedient to him, things still seem to go wrong. The disciples obeyed Jesus' instructions. He wanted to go to the other side of the lake and they immediately agreed to take him there. They were experts at the job, and they wanted to go where he directed. Yet, a 'furious squall' arose, thwarting their best intentions. This can happen in our lives, and we find it hard to cope with. We expect everything to be fine if Jesus is in the boat. If we are obeying him, living by his principles and not allowing sin to have mastery, then our expectation is that all should be well.

When events don't go according to plan, we begin to wonder if he really is 'on board', and check that we are doing his will as we thought we were. It might be that we believe that God has told us to move area, change jobs or launch a new initiative. We put decisions into motion, confident that everything will fall into place, only to find that the house won't sell, or we can't find another job, or our finances are under severe strain. That is when we question 'did God really say ...?' and feel battered and threatened by circumstances. It is also at such a point that the growing conviction of faith within us has the chance either to spurt or to shrivel up, according to our response.

Promise–problem–provision

A much misunderstood principle of growth is that of promise–problem–provision. If we can recognise this principle and the purpose in it, then our growth will be so much quicker and stronger. God gives a promise, then follows it by allowing a problem to come. Often, we think that the difficulties come from the enemy, but frequently they are actually from God – not because he wants us to suffer, but because he wants to test the strength of our commitment and faith in the promise. *Our response to the problem determines how quickly we move into our provision.* This tests us and shows us what is really in our heart.

An example of this can be seen in the Israelites and their attainment of the Promised Land. Except for Joshua and Caleb, no one from the original generation received the promise because of their response to the problem.

They would not believe that God was able, and instead grumbled and squabbled their way through the desert for forty years. The promise was still fulfilled, but through someone else. The difficulty we have is in understanding the problems of life which arise while we are obeying the Lord. Our minds fill with paralysing questions: if God is with us in the boat, how can he allow us to have a storm? Wouldn't the Father give us a break, if only for the sake of Jesus' name and reputation? Isn't the credibility of God on the line? If we tell everyone what the word of God is to us and then something goes wrong, isn't that letting his name down? Have we got the promise wrong in the first place? Did God really say . . . ?

When we have a problem, we begin to question the promise. But this is not God's way of doing things. If God said it, and you have been sure about it until this point, don't try and change it with hindsight. Believe the word, release your faith about it and remain strong even when problems arise. Never allow a problem to make you doubt the promise. We must understand that the circumstances, events and people in life that we cannot control are usually our greatest character shapers. If you want to live a significant life, then expect some significant obstacles. Problems are usually commensurate in size with the promise. *If you want a million-pound promise, then don't expect a fifty-pence-sized problem.*

Some friends of mine believed very strongly that they were being called to adopt a Romanian orphan. This was confirmed by various scriptures, prophetic words and an increasing sense of conviction and peace about it. As soon as they started to take action, though, everything seemed to conspire against them, including being told that it would be impossible because of a change in Romanian law. It would have been easy, as one obstacle followed another, to give up the idea, thinking that circumstances showed that they had got it wrong. But inside still burned the conviction that God had told them to do this and he would bring it about. Which is what eventually happened. The story is told in *Romanian Rescue* (Sue Smith, Hodder and Stoughton, 1997) and illustrates how hanging on and trusting in the middle of terrible problems does eventually bring the provision of God's promise and a growing awareness of his love and power.

Beware God's little helpers

Sometimes our potential for growth in the midst of problems is threatened by 'God's little helpers' – people who put negative pressure on you and call into question the promise of God. They emphasise the areas that are going wrong, and suggest strongly that these difficulties are God's way of telling you that you must change direction. When we last decided to move, it was not a great call of God but a commonsense need occasioned by our growing family. We were not moving away from the church, merely finding more appropriate accommodation. We felt that this was good, and were at peace about it. However, although we saw several properties that fitted our requirements, our house did not sell. At first, everyone encouraged us and prayed that it would soon sell. But as weeks slipped into months and even a year, 'God's little helpers' got into action. Those same people who at first had been so supportive now queried whether we had got it wrong. My response to their question 'Why do you think it's not selling?' was 'Because no one has bought it yet!' We did not feel any differently about moving, and eventually, of course, did manage to move. Sometimes Christians need to lighten up and stop being so intense. Superspirituality is an awful affliction and makes simple things in life unnecessarily complicated.

Christians are as much subject to the prevailing trends of everyday life as their neighbours. It's how we handle them which differs. *The way you see the problem is the problem*. In this case, we learnt and grew more through waiting than if the sale had been immediate and smooth. Weigh up what others have to say, but remain focused on the promise and purpose of God. If negative circumstances were an indication of being out of God's will, then the apostle Paul was never in his will! His life consisted of one obstacle or disaster after another – whippings, stonings, shipwrecks, imprisonment and persecution – but he kept his eyes on God and God's purposes for him. Where most of us would have retired injured after only one of these hardships, Paul shrugged them off as 'light and momentary troubles' (2 Corinthians 4:17).

The example of Abraham teaches us a great deal about growing in God when problems and setbacks beset us.

Against all hope, Abraham in hope believed and so became the father of many nations ... Without weakening in his faith, he faced the fact that his body was as good as dead – since he was about a hundred years old – and that Sarah's womb was also dead. Yet he did not waver through unbelief regarding the promise of God, but was strengthened in his faith and gave glory to God, being fully persuaded that God had power to do what he had promised.

(Romans 4:18–21)

We too can hope and believe, and so become partakers of God's promise to us. Unbelief will make us waver and will affect every area of our lives. We need, like Abraham; to be fully persuaded of God's power when the furious squall of doubt and fear tries to turn us back.

We need to stop disturbing Jesus in the boat with panicky prayers, reproaching him with 'Can't you see I'm drowning?' Don't be angry with God when you're facing a storm and he seems to be asleep. It's presumptuous to have such a bitter attitude and ascribe to him frail human characteristics. Instead, remember that God's attitude towards us is always good and pure, and that he does indeed have the power to do what he promised.

When Jesus got into the boat, it was with one purpose: 'Let us go over to the other side' (Mark 4:35). *God's expressed word is God's expressed intention*, and he could rest in the knowledge that it would come to pass. That same Creator God who has the authority to bring life into being is in our boat, and he wants us all to go over – not under – to the other side. Although Jesus may well have known about it, he never mentioned the storm, because it wasn't relevant to him. If we make it relevant to us, then we will go in the wrong direction and may even drown. If you're in a storm, don't seek Jesus for a new word on the basis that the original does not seem to be working. The storm is to test whether you believed the word in the first place. Face the fact that the circumstances are a disaster, but don't waver in unbelief. God is used to bringing order out of chaos. He will do it for us as well. We cannot speak peace to the storm until we have peace in the storm, just as Jesus had.

Promises need perseverance

Fighting through storms and overcoming obstacles to progress and growth can be exhausting. Many Christians are weary and burnt out, overwhelmed by difficult circumstances and tempted to give up altogether. Yet God wants us to see the process of gaining his promises as of equal significance to the promises themselves. Indeed, the process is an integral part of the promise: 'do not throw away your confidence; it will be richly rewarded. You need to persevere so that when you have done the will of God, you will receive what he has promised' (Hebrews 10:35).

The promise we seek is at the other side of perseverance. Perseverance is a need, as much as the goals at which we are aiming. Such a concept is not ingrained in the human mindset. We love arriving, but we despise the process of getting there. Instead, we want to take short cuts and achieve our aims instantly, both in the natural and in the spiritual. Yet process is part of the fabric of a time/space existence. God is the only one immune from process. That is why he is 'I am'. We are 'becomers', in the midst of change, and if we don't understand the need to persevere we will find ourselves faltering when circumstances or events occur which require persistence and determination.

This need for perseverance in our Christian experience was particularly highlighted to me on a recent visit to Kenya. The ethic of perseverance is much stronger in the developing world than in the West; it is more of a necessity on a daily basis, just to maintain the fundamentals of life. Because they are unable to control many aspects of existence which we take for granted, perseverance is forced upon them and becomes part of the culture. The West – including Western Christianity – is 'third world' in this aspect, and we can learn a great deal from the developing world about how to keep going in the face of almost insuperable problems in order to be nurtured and grow.

In the West, we create ways around having to wait, and invent things which do not require us to be patient or persevere about anything. It is a 'have now, pay later' culture. Everything is instant – food, drink, finance, travel, excitement, beauty, health – and the idea of perseverance is not only misunderstood, it is unwelcome. The pace of life has speeded up immeasurably in the past decades, and while much of the progress has been helpful and positive, it has certainly undermined our ability to persevere. Because so many elements of life – water, light, heat, food, clothing, transport and communications – come to us easily and without much effort on our part, we have lost the habit of working hard at reaching for things we cannot easily command.

Christians have fallen into the same mindset. We avoid, or react badly to, anything we can't control, blaming the enemy, because we can't equate negative circumstances with the kind of God we thought we were believing in when we came to Christ. Many people have believed that Christianity is an inoculation from problems, but this is plainly not true. Among the many wonderful promises of God is the rarely quoted 'In this world you will have trouble' (John 16:33). It is as much a promise as any of the more popular ones, and what's more, it is regularly fulfilled! If you want to do anything significant with your life, if there is any way in which you want to stand out from the crowd, then trouble will come looking for you. However, this is not necessarily an attack from an enemy to bring us down. Much of the trouble we encounter is to strengthen the ethic of perseverance, for life requires us to learn how to persist so that, when we attain what we are seeking in life, our hands do not become careless in handling that which came to us at great cost.

When I first met with churches in Kenya, I was frustrated by people's extreme lateness. Some were still arriving over an hour after the beginning of the meeting, and it could be very disruptive and distracting. Then I discovered the reason for the lateness and my frustration evaporated. No one had their own vehicles and so the people were dependent upon public transport, which is very different from our understanding of the term. The main means of transport was not bus, train or taxi, but *matatoos*, clapped-out old mini-buses which waited until they were full before even setting off and then took on more and more passengers along the way. Overloaded and poorly maintained, they often broke down, and many hours were spent with driver and passengers alike attempting to do makeshift repairs. Late-comers, therefore, were merely victims of a totally inadequate infrastructure over which they had no control. They travelled many miles, setting off extremely early in order to come to the meeting, but even then were late because so much of the journey was out of their hands.

It is difficult for us in the West to imagine living like that, nor should we necessarily applaud a way of life which produces so much unnecessary hardship, but it also produces a determination and enthusiasm which is a shining example to us. Africans think nothing of putting themselves out considerably in order to worship God together, and this is a lesson to us spoilt Western Christians who complain if there's a puddle in the car park. Comfort-zone Christians have no concept of that sort of persistence. Through my observations in Kenya, God reminded me of the need of perseverance in our journey through life with him.

I saw women in the tea plantations picking their fingers to the bone for 60p a day. I saw people by the roadside who spent all day trying to sell ten bananas. We passed two small boys, with no shoes on, pushing a large sack of maize on a home-made wheelbarrow up a long, muddy hill. It would have taken them an entire day just to go to market, buy the maize and then get it back to their village. Our children here would have no concept of that sort of time commitment to a task. They would be horrified at the thought. An old man knelt near the roadside, planting grass to feed his terribly gaunt cow enough for her to produce a tiny amount of milk. That was the endless cycle of his life, encompassed by a few square metres of baked land. Perhaps most heart-rending of all was the sight of two ladies chipping away at huge boulders with home-made lump hammers. They were breaking the rocks up into hard core for construction work. It would take them about a week to produce enough to sell, and yet they had no assured buyer. They were labouring in hope, determined to do something to help towards the family needs. Such dogged determination made me realise afresh the possibilities for perseverance within our own lives and the huge opportunities for growth it provides.

Persistence overcomes resistance The simple truth is that if you do not quit, you can win. Conversely, if you do quit, you will never win. If we persevere, we will receive the promise. The enemy has not got enough ammunition to destroy us if every day we get up and say to ourselves, 'Today, I *will* continue. I will not give up.' We never know how close we are to the breakthrough we are seeking. We never know when the promise will be fulfilled or when the change in our circumstances will come. So many people let go when only a breath away from fulfilment. Far better to follow the encouragement in Galatians: 'Let us not become weary in doing good, for at the proper time we will reap a harvest if we do not give up' (Galatians 6:9). No one knows when the 'proper time' is, so we need to be ready, not giving up but hanging on tenaciously to what we believe. There comes a point in cycling up a hill when the cyclist has to stand on the pedals and really put a lot of effort into going forward. If he stopped at this point he would lose ground and might even wobble and fall off. The moment we cease to decide to go forward, other laws automatically take over. But *if we stand on the pedals of our life and persevere, we will get over the hill* we are facing and then be able to see the wonderful view as we cruise down the other side.

Perseverance turns problems into blessings The Bible is a book of second efforts. It is full of characters such as Moses, David, Peter and Saul of Tarsus who were given another chance by God. He does not make failures, he creates winners. Failure is not to have tried and come short, it is the refusal to try at all. *Life is a grindstone, and whether it polishes you or destroys you depends on what you are made of.* The problems we encounter can make us shine like diamonds if we are determined to overcome them and not let them overcome us.

Perseverance breeds confidence The more you persevere, the more you gain in strength and self-belief and the more you become convinced that you have within you the resources to fight the next battle. The Israelites said that Goliath was too big to beat, and gave up trying. David, though, looked at it a different way and declared that Goliath was too big to miss. His earlier overcoming of lion and bear gave him confidence that with God on his side, he could do it (1 Samuel 17:37). The fact that he had progressed through earlier challenges meant that he was ready for this much bigger one.

In horticulture and agriculture there is a season of perseverance: the season between sowing and reaping, a time of growth, where the gardener or farmer is fighting bugs, keeping pests at bay and uprooting weeds. What is growing is assaulted, and it takes perseverance to protect it. The same is true in our spiritual lives. Jim Rohn, a secular motivational writer, states that

> Success in life is not an easy matter, nor is it an easy matter for the seed to push its way through the soil in its quest to find the light and the airborne chemicals

which give it health ... Life is designed to be a story of achievement in spite of adversity, not the absence of adversity, for without adversity, achievement could not exist ... Does the seed complain because of the rocks it must grow over, under, around or through? ... The only automatic things in life are weeds and bugs ... Expect adversity for it shall surely appear. Be grateful for adversity for it forces the human spirit to grow, for surely the human character is formed not in the absence of difficulty but in our response to difficulty.

(*The Seasons of Life*, Jim Rohn Int., 1981)

Don't quit

There are many examples of notable people who would have deprived the world of a great deal if they had given up when faced with problems and rejection. Fred Astaire failed his first screen test in 1933. He was told, 'You can't act, you can't sing, you're slightly bald, and you can dance a little.' The famous opera singer Enrico Caruso was told by his singing teacher that he could not sing to save his life, and to consider other careers. Walt Disney was fired from his newspaper job for lack of ideas. Einstein did not speak until he was four years old, and did not read until he was seven. He was described by his teacher as 'mentally slow, a foolish dreamer', and was eventually expelled from school and refused entry to Zurich Polytechnic. Winston Churchill failed his A levels and did not become Prime Minister until the age of sixty-two. Abraham Lincoln failed twelve times to become

President of the United States, and spent thirty-two years of his life trying. He had a huge track record of utter failure in business, politics and in his personal life. At last, in 1860, he was elected President, and many say he was the best that America ever had. Describing his life, he said: 'My path was worn and my path was slippery. My foot slipped from under me many times, and at the same time knocked from under me my other foot. But I recovered and said to myself "it's a slip and not a fall".' If Abraham Lincoln, who never claimed to be a Christian or to walk in the power of the Holy Spirit which is available to us, could spend so long failing and still persevere, how much more can we.

Most of the valuable things in history, that we take for granted now – inventions, both scientific and medical progress, new laws and freedoms – have been achieved through obstacles, setbacks, heartache and rejection, breeding a perseverance that we need to emulate. We must commit to this ethic and speak of it with conviction rather than skirt round the subject, afraid that it will put people off. We must not give non-Christians the impression that being a Christian is a trouble-free life, for that certainly is not our experience!

God is not Santa Claus

A middle-aged man came as a visitor to our church, having apparently been told that all his problems would be solved because Jesus was the answer. This man came up to me at the end of a service, and asked, 'Are you the pastor here?'

Despite my immediate instinct to deny that I even knew the pastor, I replied, 'Yes, I am.'

He then issued me with an ultimatum, saying, 'I was told that you people would sort everything out for me. I've been coming here for three Sunday mornings and things are getting worse. My wife has left me, my business has collapsed, my house has been repossessed and now I am on medication for stress and depression.' His punch line followed: 'I am giving you one more week, and at the end of that week, if you haven't sorted things out, I am leaving.'

My response was immediate. I said, 'Sir, let me shake your hand and say goodbye now. Let me release both of us from an awful week ahead.'

I then asked him how old he was. He replied, 'I'm fifty-four.'

I said, 'You have taken fifty-four years to get your life into this mess and you're giving God a week. I don't think so. Here's my offer to you: give us a year of your life, follow our advice, and at the end of it you will be a different man.'

His reply, like the rich young ruler's to Jesus, was saddening. 'No,' he said, 'that's far too much to ask of me.' He turned and walked away and I never saw him again. We must stop telling people that God is some kind of heavenly Santa Claus. God is a father, and fathers operate by relationship, not demands and ultimatums.

We need to understand that obstacles and problems are an integral and valuable part of life. Too many Christians behave as if they want a refund from God or the church because the small print about problems was never mentioned. Our role model is Jesus, and we need to throw off everything that hinders [us] and the sin that so easily entangles, and let us run with perseverance the race marked out for us. Let us fix our eyes on Jesus, the author and perfecter of our faith, who for the joy set before him endured the cross, scorning its shame, and sat down at the right hand of the throne of God. Consider him who endured such opposition from sinful men, so that you will not grow weary and lose heart.

(Hebrews 12:1–3)

As we follow this advice and tackle problems with determination and God's perspective on them, we will develop in character, relationships, maturity and intimacy with God. We will indeed learn how to stay strong when it all goes wrong.

Let the weak say, 'I am strong'

'Let the weak say, I am strong' was the great prophetic proclamation of Joel to a beleaguered Israel (Joel 3:10 King James Version). Persistent weakness of a particular kind is the enemy of progress and growth. There are two types of weakness described in the Bible. The apostle Paul mentions one type when he says that God's 'power is made perfect in weakness' (2 Corinthians 12:9). This is the weakness of limitation and inadequacy, of insufficiency outside Christ. This is the weakness that drives us into God and keeps us dependent on him. The other type, which is the one referred to by Joel, is translated by the Hebrew word *challâsh*, which means frail, feeble, easily overcome. This is an almost self-indulgent, continual weakness, for which no change or help is sought because the weak person has learnt to live with their weakness and doesn't actually want to become strong. Paul's weakness glorifies God; *challâsh* does not.

Gideon is an example of someone with a chronic case of *challâsh* . He lived during a low point in Israel's history, when the enemy had the upper hand and were system-atically oppressing the Israelites. This constant wearing down by the enemy had undermined their relationship with the Lord. Gideon's first response to the angel of the Lord is 'but', followed closely by 'if', 'why?' and 'where?' (Judges 6:12). He was so established in a mindset of weakness that he argued with the Lord's angel.

Challâsh disorientates us, so that we miss God when he's actually there speaking to us. We're too caught up with the baggage of our weakness. Confession of this kind of weakness is the overflow of an underlying reservoir of unbelief, doubt and negativity. It gathers its own vocabulary that is contrary to the large-thinking, vast-possibility language of the Holy Spirit.

Challâsh refuses to receive strength. It is addictive. Gideon was told that the Lord was with him, but he did not believe it. Instead, he tried to drag the angel down into a discussion about weakness. God's response to this is amazing: 'Go in the strength you have and save Israel out of Midian's hand. Am I not sending you?' (Judges 6:14). But this was not what Gideon, in his perception of his own weakness, wanted to hear. His reply to God's encouragement and command ran along the lines of: 'Didn't you hear a thing I just said? Are you not aware of the depth of my frustration and agony, which I just tried to express to you? I have no strength to go anywhere with.' Never interpret God's ignoring of something you tell him as deafness. There is no need to keep telling God about the same things, because it only makes you frustrated and angry. He hears the first time, but his interest lies in your response to what he is telling you. He already knows all that you are telling him, and can help if you will listen. But he will not enter into the problem. He is too large for that. He is much more likely to tell you to stop whining, move out of weakness and go in the strength you have.

Gideon then lists all his weaknesses, still trying to put God right. He is sure that God can't mean him. He must have got the wrong man. The next stage after thinking the Lord has ignored you is to tell him that he's got it wrong. Moses also reacted in this way and told God that he was mistaken when he chose him to speak to Pharaoh (Exodus 3 and 4). It's easy to judge Gideon and Moses and wonder at their daring in arguing with the mighty God, but we also, at times, disqualify ourselves for the work he has called us to do. We mustn't think like this, because everyone is needed in a time of harvest. And if God has called us, then he will equip us for the task (2 Peter 1:3).

Strength is not a secret. We can all learn how to look to God for strength. And if we all did, imagine what the church would be like if all those paralysed by *challâsh* were suddenly set free and started to become strong. There would be a massive release of resources in terms of the time, energy, emotion and practical help which are currently spent 'in-house'. Many, many more people would be saved, delivered and healed. God gives us strength to reach the world, and shows us how to turn the tools of weakness into weapons of warfare. In the words of the prophet Joel, 'Beat your ploughshares into swords and your pruning hooks into spears. Let the weakling say, "I am strong!" ' (Joel 3:10).

Key Points

- Our reponse to the problem determines how quickly we move into our provision.

- If you want a million-pound promise, then don't expect a fifty-pence-sized problem.

- The way you see the problem is the problem.

- God's expressed word is God's expressed intention.

- If we stand on the pedals of our life and persevere, we will get over the hill.

- Life is a grindstone, and whether it polishes you or destroys you depends on what you are made of.

4

Why isn't my church growing?

If you had planted an expensive shrub in the garden and, some time later, noticed that it was obviously not flourishing, your first reaction would probably not be to fall on your knees and beg God to reveal the reason why this plant was not progressing well! It is more likely that you would examine it for signs of infestation or disease, you would look at the soil to see if it was rich and moist enough, and you would check the instructions that came with the shrub to make sure that you had planted it in the right place, with the correct nutrients and enough sun or shade. It is usually quite apparent what the problem is, and relatively straightforward to fix it.

It is no different when examining church growth. There are no mysteries as to why a church isn't growing. The problem is more often getting the people in that church, especially the leaders, to face the issues and address them. Growth is not difficult if we can find out what people want and present it in a way that is inoffensive, accessible and attractive. Sadly for much of the church in our country, the refusal to change things that hinder growth remains the abiding difficulty. It is simply not enough to want to grow, or be eloquent in articulating growth principles, or even have a passion for the lost. I know of many churches about whom this is true, and yet they are also unwilling to change, whether change means relocating to a more user-friendly building, adjustments in the style of public meetings for the sake of those unused to 'church', changing religious jargon, or changing the people in charge.

Unless churches are willing to examine themselves honestly and radically in response to the vital question of why they aren't growing, then the question is futile. I have visited numerous churches where the reason for their lack of growth was painfully evident the moment you walked in. It's called unfriendliness! The problem is that every church thinks it is friendly – and usually is within its own closed circle of members. My wife and I have visited churches where no one greeted us, asked our names or showed any interest in us whatsoever. And yet these same churches are burning the midnight oil in prayer for revival. Why is it that many Christians would sooner pray and fast for their church to grow than simply learn to be friendly? In our church, we ask visitors, by way of a response card, to tell us what they think of us. I always look for the words 'warm', 'friendly' and 'welcoming' on those cards. Nine times out of ten that is what people say about us, but nine times out of ten is still not good enough. Friendliness in the church is never coincidental; it is the result of friendly leadership and a constant effort to ensure that the church stays that way.

Through the keyhole

Growing churches should be like growing cities. When you live in or even visit certain cities, you can very quickly sense whether or not they are growing. New road systems under construction; new buildings of all kinds going up everywhere; national and international companies choosing to be based there; corporate head offices being established there; bigger, better, more prestigious events being hosted by the city, with increased tourism as a result – all these things speak of a place alive with growth-related activity. Growing churches are just the same. You can tell the moment you walk in whether an environment and atmosphere of growth is present or not. A dilapidated building, threadbare carpets, a damp musky smell, peeling paint everywhere and dated décor do not speak of an atmosphere of growth. Cobwebs around doors and window frames, cheesy religious posters and various other religious regalia randomly scattered across the building do not speak of growth and forward thinking. These church buildings are simply an extension, an echo, of the people who use them. Buildings, equipment and furnishings all speak far louder than we realise of the kind of people who use them. I have often wondered what Lloyd Grosman would say about some church buildings if the programme *Through the Keyhole* sent him to ask the question 'Who lives in a house like this?' Would he conclude that a well-organised, contemporary, forward-looking and attractive people must live here? Or would he assume that it must be an old pre-war Victorian film set, reconstructed for some period drama?

Atmosphere and environment

We must understand that it is not enough to speak about growth, increase and change while nothing around us reflects it. A church committed to growth must understand the need to embody that commitment in both its vocabulary and its appearance. *We need to understand and harness to our advantage the power of atmosphere and environment.* They are two of the most neglected aspects of church life. Environment and atmosphere are the surrounding conditions which can directly influence the desired outcomes that we want in people's lives. Walk into any major department store like Harvey Nichols, Selfridges or even Marks and Spencer; look past the products and try to tune in to the surrounding subliminal stimuli – lighting, décor, aromas, music, colour co-ordination, placement of mirrors, windows, potted plants. Creating the correct environment has become a science in its own right, and one that pays people large sums of money to ensure standards of perfection.

In my own home church we have an ACTS team. ACTS stands for Atmosphere Co-ordination Team. These few, specially chosen people are responsible for creating the right surrounding atmosphere every time our building is hosting a major event. They give attention to background music, lighting levels, the aesthetic appearance of room layouts, colour co-ordination, positioning of the plants and foliage, tidiness of notice boards and information desks, etc. *Atmosphere is the invisible packaging of the element we most want people to sense and receive.* You may have the right product, but if it is poorly presented then the response will be limited. I appeal to churches everywhere to give attention to these hidden but vital elements. The apostle Paul said that 'by all means' we should win some, and if giving attention to the atmosphere and environment of our church building contributes to that, then we should not neglect it.

Stay God-centred!

The chief purpose of the church is to glorify God, and to 'go and make disciples of all nations, baptising them in the name of the Father and of the Son and of the Holy Spirit and teaching them to obey everything I have commanded you' (Matthew 28:19–20). In order to fulfil such a demanding aim, it is essential that God is at the very centre of all we do. If he is not at the centre, then really, we're all wasting our time. Whatever our centre is in life determines what we'll give our life to, and although we might say, and indeed believe, that God is at the centre, too often he slips to the periphery as something else takes precedence.

When Paul wrote to the church at Colossae, it was in an effort to refocus the people on Jesus. The church was drifting from its centre, riddled with heresies and strange philosophies which were undermining its struggle to establish roots. The people were distracted and diverted, and that is a danger for all of us. Paul urges them to remember who is central:

> For everything, absolutely everything, above and below, visible and invisible, rank after rank of angels – everything got started in him and finds its purpose in

him. He was there before any of it came into existence and holds it all together right up to this moment. And when it comes to the church, he organises it and holds it together, like a head does a body.

(Colossians 1:15–23, *Message* Version)

Knowing your centre is essential – then every other line of reference finds its place. When you move from your centre, every other line becomes blurred and boundaries shift. Mental hospitals and prisons are full of people who have lost their centre and have become disorientated as a result. *The difference between a pilgrim and a wanderer – and both inhabit the church – is that one has a centre and one doesn't.* The distinction is demonstrated essentially in lifestyle. Once God is central in the heart, it's not difficult to find him in every other area of life, past, present and future.

In every single generation since the church was born, the issue of God-centredness has had to be addressed. The danger in the recent moves of restoration and re-freshing, such as the 'Toronto blessing' and others, is that they breed a kind of complacency among some, a feeling that the church has finally matured and all emphasis should now be on evangelism. However, my observation is that by and large, throughout the UK and beyond, much of the church hasn't changed as a consequence of this recent move of God. Many who jumped from traditional, non-charismatic backgrounds into what God was doing have returned to those same traditional religious practices and abandoned the things that the move of God came to re-centre or restore to them. Also, many other churches from a more charismatic background have failed to take hold of any new focus God was bringing, and instead have reverted to type. The message of a God-centred church is more needed now, as we start a new millennium, than ever before.

The true church is where Christ is supreme in absolutely everything which that church does, thinks, believes, reaches for, builds and plans. Such a church will be Christ-besotted, Christ-embracing, Christ-exporting. The theory sounds wonderful – surely we all ascribe to it without reservation? The practice, however, proves to be more difficult.

Here are seven alternatives to a God-centred church. If a church fits into one of these categories, or is in danger of doing so, then it will not grow to its full potential, for the ingredients for fruitful positive growth are lacking, submerged by other, more hostile elements.

The church-centred church The people in this church are focused upon themselves, spending many hours 'navel-gazing' and commenting introspectively. The emphasis is need-orientated, and heavily into counselling. Problems are uppermost in speech and prayer, and the pastoral system is used too extensively. Such a church is in love with the method of worship and not with the person they are worshipping, the way they do things rather than who they are doing it for. There are many unresolved problems, because the problems are not being taken to the place where they will be properly sorted out: Jesus, not the pastoral team. Jesus is the only person in the Bible referred to as 'wonderful counsellor', yet few go to him for counsel. Sometimes the best thing we can say when people ask for help is 'no' and instead encourage them to seek God first. I was once phoned up in the dead of night by a lady who wanted me to come over immediately to cast out a 'demonic presence' which she was convinced was in the house. I refused and gently encouraged her to do something about it herself. At the time she was hurt and upset by my refusal. Yet later she testified that it was the best thing that had ever happened to her. She learnt to turn to God instead of man. A church-centred church has lots of tensions and 'fall-outs' because it is concentrated on the people and their needs and agendas, instead of on the Lord and his purpose. It is infatuated with trivia rather than the tremendous, magnifying small issues and giving them a false importance. There is competitiveness, boredom and cliquishness. Many Christians are bored with church because they have stopped seeking the kingdom. The church can only function properly when she springs from a vital pursuit of his kingdom

The tradition-centred church This is where traditions, whatever they might be, are top priority. It may be a tradition of language, a whole religious vocabulary, jargon, of which we are unaware. We speak so differently that we are out of touch with how the rest of the world talks. We're not connecting with those who so desperately want to know answers to fundamental questions. Most people do not have the courage to ask what we mean when they don't understand. They are just put off. Then we wonder why we're not growing. Style, rules, dress, appearance – not of themselves significant, yet often possessing undue significance in our church lives – can all be dictated by tradition. Strangers feel on the outside and unwelcome if they do not fit in with our particular 'style'. Even Bible-based traditions can be obstacles if the way we've always done something, such as Communion, becomes more important than the people it was meant for. As Jesus pointed out to his own traditionalists, 'the Sabbath was made for man, not man for the Sabbath' (Mark 2:27). People are God's most important creation, and if we as a church make tradition, methods or style more important than the people we are reaching, then we are not Christ-centred and we will not grow. *Tradition-centredness forces conformity at the expense of freedom.* It is married to methods, constitutions and committees, and they are in control rather than the Spirit of God. We need to examine our traditions and see if they need adjusting. Are we traditional in our worship, length of meeting, various ministries or seating plan? Revival is not in spite of us; we have got to be ready for what God is going to do, equipped and prepared to get the job done. A church which is more absorbed with the outward form than inner relationship, and expects all its new converts to take that on board too, burdening them from the beginning with baggage which God never intended them to have, will simply not grow.

The reaction-centred church This is the group that sets something up in the town as a reaction to another church. It is not Christ-centred, nor mission-centred, for it has no call, no vision and no mandate from God. The common denominator of all its people, the ethos driving them to create the group in the first place, is a reaction, a bad attitude to another church or its leadership. God is then 'bolted on' to this basis, to give it a spurious authority. Three such groups have just collapsed in this area, and it's a tragedy. While it lasts, the group causes trouble, and when it folds, many lives are damaged. It usually takes two to three years to run its course; God does not bless it, for his hand is not on it. If something is born out of reaction, it can never, ever, be God-centred. Reaction is in the root, and becomes part of the weave of its life. Reaction must be dealt with and repented of before Christ can be truly central again. It is impossible to build a foundation of love upon a foundation of hate. And it is impossible to build upon a foundation of hate and call it God. The Lord did not honour Moses when he tried to anticipate God's purposes by killing an Egyptian. Because that was a reaction, not God-centred, he had to wait forty years to do it God's way. Peter reacted rather than followed Jesus' lead when he cut off the servant's ear, wanting to fight against those who opposed his master. Jesus, however, restored the man's ear, thereby refusing to be part of this reaction. *Leaders, like Jesus, must not become involved with something which begins and is therefore rooted in reaction.* Beware of publicly opposing such groups in your vicinity. They already have the seeds of self-destruction in them. Be faithful to individuals; warn them of their vulnerability if you meet them, but otherwise leave it alone. Just recently, two people came to me acknowledging that they had got it wrong and that our warnings to them had been right. I'm more than happy to receive them back into the church, providing that both the original issue that made them react and their tendency to react and walk out are properly resolved.

The leadership-limitation centred church This is the church where the leader does not have the capacity to take it forward, but is not strong enough to step aside to allow someone else to take over. Because of his position, everybody gets locked into his limitation. This is actually quite a serious situation for a church to be in, and yet many are in it. It is not in any way that the leader is of no use to God or the church, just that he would function more effectively and happily in a different role. How difficult, though, for someone to admit this, and give up status, income perhaps, and self-regard. How wonderful if he were able to say, 'I just don't believe that God has given me the grace and gifting to take the church forward to the next phase. Therefore, I've asked those close to me to pray about repositioning me elsewhere in the church and placing someone else into the leadership to take the church on.' Unsurprisingly, perhaps, this rarely happens. Once, when I was in Canada, I was asked to pray over some pastors, not having met them or spoken with them at all. I knew, therefore, that anything I said or prayed would have to be from God, since I was totally ignorant of situations or personalities. It was exciting and daunting at the same time! I laid hands on one of these pastors and immediately had a picture in my mind of him at a garage, complaining to the mechanic that he had had four sets of brake pads fitted on his car that year. In my picture, the mechanic replied that it wasn't his fault, that the owner was too hard on the brakes and needed to ease off them. When I described this, the pastor and his wife laughed in amazement, but I noticed that some of the congregation were near to tears. The amazement was because the exact situation had occurred the previous day, when the pastor went to collect his car from the garage. I prophesied that God was telling him to ease off the brakes on the church, to let it move forward without jerking it back by being controlling and over-cautious. The pastor chose to ignore this word from God, and later I heard that within six months the church had collapsed. The man was not big enough to take his foot off the brake and allow the church to move forward at its maximum speed. Many churches are in similar situations, locked into small leaders doing jobs which are too big for them and therefore limited to that leader's faith, rule and anointing.

The programme-centred church This is a busy, sometimes frenetic church, crammed with events, meetings and plans and requiring a huge financial budget to cover them all. The programme is often much bigger than the church itself, and becomes the centre of the life of the church. I have observed this to be a particular issue in America, where there is much competition between programme-centred churches, but I foresee it becoming an increasing problem in Britain as well. One event follows another relentlessly, and people are sustained by the programme, often leaving the church if there is a lull or the programme is not to their liking. All of the various ministries in the programme, good though they are, often serve to cover lacks in the resident leadership. Visiting speakers, 'big names', will draw crowds, create a 'feel-good' factor, and yet still disguise an inner lack on the part of the local congregation. Of course, there is always a need for a vibrant agenda in the church, but this must be supplementary rather than primary.

The building-centred church This church is locked into its building, focusing on the literal, physical structure rather than the people. Sometimes, the building is historical, and then there is a link with traditionalism as well. For others, it is more a case of over-centralisation and dependence on the building and all its resources, including staff. This can stifle initiative for people in their everyday lives, as they develop a mentality that everything must be building- or meeting-based. A 'come to' rather than a 'go to' mindset is fostered, and people do not consider what they can do in their own neighbourhoods and workplaces to share Jesus. Church life majors on the gathering at the expense of the church in the community.

The movement-centred church Some churches follow all the latest ministry personalities and moves of God, such as Toronto, Pensacola and Argentina. I thank God for them all, but some people travel across the world in an effort to try to discover that elusive key that will lead to revival in their town. They have a wonderful time and then come back to reproduce what they have seen in their own churches. But these centres are not models to be copied, they're signs from God. The move of God is unique and tailor-made for wherever you are. It's marvellous to go to be inspired and encouraged, but not to take home a stencil for trying to produce an exact copy. It is fruitless to look for a formula from them, because it won't work. A movement-centred church always abandons everything to take on board the latest, popular spiritual trend. It's good to draw from all that God is doing in the world, but ensure that the church remains Christ-centred. In that way, you're 'plugged in' to the movement behind every movement.

These alternatives represent a very real danger for every church if it allows its focus to slip from the Lord himself. Loss of God-centredness will inevitably lead to stagnation in the church, and an impeding of God's purposes for it.

The power of combination punching

Recently, while I sat in Belfast airport waiting for my return flight to England, something happened through which I knew God was wanting to get my attention and tell me something. In the relatively small and almost empty airport lounge, a man came walking in wearing a tracksuit and baseball cap. He suddenly adjusted his stride, stood still and punched the air with a volley of punches, and then calmly carried on walking. After him followed several other men, all of whom did exactly the same thing. It became evident from the back of their tracksuits that they were members of a boxing club. In the seconds following this impromptu demonstration, the Holy Spirit whispered the phrase 'combination punching' into my heart.

It wasn't until later that same evening that the full impact of this phrase came home to me. I arrived early at our church building to speak at our Sunday evening service, where the baptism of twenty of our new believers was already going on in another hall. The hall was packed with about two hundred people, a good sixty of whom were first-time visitors, there to watch the various families and friends being baptised. During the next thirty minutes, I began to pray for these visitors to be touched and influenced positively by the event. At this point the Holy Spirit brought that boxing team back to my mind with these words: 'It's the power of combination punching.' God began to show me that everything works by combination, especially people coming to know Christ. God told me that these visitors were under a barrage of combination punches and that he wanted me

76

to deliver the final blow when I preached that evening. Of those that stayed on for our evening service, seventeen came to Christ, and many of them completed family units by doing so.

Within the space of three hours these unsaved, unsuspecting visitors were exposed to a winning combination of friendship, hospitality, testimony, devotion and finally the preaching of the word of God and the necessity of a decision from them.

A combination is a series of numbers that must be dialled in order to open a lock. I've begun to see that God operates by the power of combinations to unlock people's lives. Our failure to understand this means that we fumble around trying to find that one knock-out blow that we can deliver. Many churches put all their efforts into an 'all eggs in one basket' type of event, expecting it to achieve results that only come by a combination of things. We want to hit and run, when God wants us to stay and deliver well-chosen combinations of overwhelming 'blows'.

A while ago, I was talking to a pastor who told me that their second Alpha programme was poor compared to the first. His perceptive suggestion as to the reason for this was that they had separated out the new converts from the first Alpha programme into a separate class, while trying to start a second Alpha on another night with all their family and friends. It didn't work. Their friends didn't come. This local church leadership had unwittingly interfered with a divine combination – that is, that they had separated the fruit from their immediate seed. Genesis 1:11 tells us that God made fruit with seed in it, and every new convert has the seed of the next batch in their lives. Our baptism service had them both in the same room, the fruit getting baptised and their seed watching them. The Alpha courses in our country have tapped into a winning combination: food, friendship, witness. This simple one-two-three has proved to be an overwhelmingly successful combination.

For this principle to work, the church must first understand other, more subliminal combination requirements.

Positional combinations

Combinations of position are usually orchestrated by God, as Paul told the gathered crowd in Athens:

> From one man he made every nation of men, that they should inhabit the whole earth; and he determined the times set for them and the exact places where they should live. God did this so that men would seek him and perhaps reach out for him and find him, though he is not far from each one of us.
>
> (Acts 17:26–7)

Paul suggests that throughout the ages God has divinely orchestrated the positioning of people, even down to the exact places where they would live. Then God has further ensured that each person's world would be provided with sufficient opportunity to find him. God positions people exactly, to ensure that the right people are in the right place at the right time, so that they are then available to be exposed to a series of secondary combinations like the one Alpha operates. God positioned the Ethiopian eunuch, then positioned Philip to arrive at the perfect time to interpret a perfect passage of scripture that the Ethiopian eunuch was reading at that exact time. God orchestrated both the gathering of the apostles in the upper room and the one outside in Jerusalem's streets to which they would speak. God set up Peter's visit to Cornelius with a series of well-timed combination punches of positioning. The problem has often been that while God has done his bit in divinely positioning people, the church has been sadly lagging behind in dialling the final digits of the combination to achieve breakthrough in people's lives.

The power of combination is evident in business, sport, the arts and show business. We see what happens when a winning combination is broken up in a team sport, a company, or even pop groups and comedy duos. Some things just belong together, and we separate them to our detriment. In chemistry, certain elements are brought together and merged by heat into a compound. This synthesis then becomes an unlocking combination, releasing the various properties within those elements which would otherwise remain inaccessible. *Every heart and life is guarded by a combination lock, but God is the master locksmith of the universe.* Some people's combinations can be quite complex, yet all have common digits in their code. Love, friendship, grace and understanding will touch everyone. It's the goodness of God which begins to unlock and lead people to repentance.

Some people's locks are on a timer, just like a safe. I have known families in which every member except one came to Christ, where this last one took months or even years to come to the faith. For some mysterious reason their lock was on a timer. I've often heard people say that they didn't know why they didn't respond before – somehow they just didn't feel the time was right. If you have a loved one or a friend who seems to be on a timer lock, resist the temptation to use dynamite to speed things up. Trying to 'blast' them with clumsy attempts to set them up in manufactured situations will do more harm than good, and could even further delay the timer from activating.

The importance of closure

Closure is a business term. It means to clinch the deal to get the order. I spent many years in sales prior to coming into full-time ministry, and we all knew that closure separated the men from the boys. It didn't matter how good you were in talking about the product or how winsome you were with the customers, the issue was whether or not you could close the deal. Sometimes I would go into a place only hours after a competitor salesman had been in, and I would come out with the order that he had wanted. On one such occasion, I remember asking the customer, 'Why didn't you give the order to the other salesman? He was here first.' I will never forget his answer: 'The other guy never asked me to buy it.' I believe that the vast majority of Christians who do share their faith are prone to be long on talk and short on closure.

Jesus operated with a simple three-punch combination: preaching, teaching and healing. With these three elements, he went around touching not only people's minds, but their bodies too. Jesus brought closure to people's lives. Wherever he taught, he would heal in combination with the teaching, and whenever he healed, he would teach or preach in combination with the healing. He knew that for people to find closure he had to offer them something for spirit, soul and body, and this three-punch combination did exactly that.

The apostle Peter was just getting into the swing of his introduction when the Holy Spirit brought closure to Cornelius and his household (Acts 10:44). In contrast, the apostle Paul, when standing before King Agrippa at the court of Governor Festus, moved so quickly to closure that the king was recorded as saying to Paul, 'Do you think that in such a short time you can persuade me to be a Christian?' Paul's reply is a classic closure mentality comment. 'Short time or long – I pray God that not only you but all who are listening to me today may become what I am' (Acts 26:29).

Christians are weak on closure. We tell ourselves that people aren't ready; we don't want to be too pushy. The truth is that, right now, as you're reading this, the Mormons and the Jehovah's Witnesses are getting closure. Right now, double-glazing and car salesmen are getting closure. Why? Because they are simply asking people for a decision. You would be surprised how open people are to the offer of closure. Jesus didn't hesitate. 'You must be born again,' he said. Peter, at Pentecost, also didn't hesitate, or reply to the question 'What shall we do?' with 'Well, come back next week when I start my series on repentance.' He said, 'Repent, be baptised and receive the Holy Spirit.' In other words, he achieved closure.

The strong-shouldered church

The power of a punch is in the shoulder, and shoulders in the Bible speak of government, rule, strength and power. You can tell a great deal by people's shoulders. Drooping, sagging or stooped shoulders all speak of a burdened, heavy, depressive outlook. Many Christians and even whole churches can display this sagging-shoulders appearance, as if they are carrying the cares and burdens of the world on their shoulders. We must have strong spiritual shoulders if we are to pack the kind of punch required to help people come to Christ. Many churches are not growing because they have weak, over-burdened shoulders. Their witness is anaemic and diluted, and though they say the right things, they lack the power either to sustain a combination of punches or to produce sufficient power for the punches to count. Make sure your shoulders are free from things you shouldn't be carrying. 'Cast all your anxiety upon him because he cares for you,' Peter said (1 Peter 5:7). God wants a strong-shouldered church, for there is power in the shoulders.

There are so many reasons why a church may not be growing, many of them simple and easily dealt with. This chapter, while by no means extensive, offers some suggestions, useful pointers and practical advice on this subject of lack of growth, growth that is so earnestly desired, yet sometimes apparently so unattainable.

Key Points

- We need to understand and harness to our advantage the power of atmosphere and environment.

- Atmosphere is the invisible packaging of the element we most want people to see and receive.

- The difference between a pilgrim and a wanderer – and both inhabit the church – is that one has a centre and one doesn't.

- Tradition-centredness forces conformity at the expense of freedom.

- Leaders, like Jesus, must not become involved with something which begins and is therefore rooted in reaction.

- Every heart and life is guarded by a combination lock, but God is the master locksmith of the universe.

- Jesus operated with a simple three-punch combination: preaching, teaching and healing.

5

Big is beautiful

It was hard to believe, like so many of our experiences
during this first visit to California. Here we were, on a
freeway on a Sunday morning, stuck in a traffic jam. It
was as if it was rush hour during the week. And why
had traffic ground to a halt on what should be a quiet
morning on the roads? The cars were all making their
way to an impressive-looking building set back a little
from the road. It was Saddleback Valley Community
Church in Mission Viejo, California, and thousands of
people were converging on it for the Sunday service. It
is, of course, a truism that America does everything
bigger and more flamboyantly than Britain, and most of
the time we are quite thankful to maintain the difference.
But should we feel like that about their churches? Do we
dismiss such churches of thousands as merely social and
superficial, with plenty of razzmatazz but no depth?
Should we not instead be dreaming of a time when the
roads round *our* buildings are blocked because of the
numbers trying to get there? If we believe that the Lord
wants to bring as many as will into relationship with him,
then we must accept that large churches are inevitable.

If I had a pound for every time I have heard someone

say, 'Numbers don't matter – it is quality that God wants,' I would be rich by now. If numbers don't matter then why does scripture say so much about them? Why does it tell us that there were 120 in the upper room, or that three thousand were saved at Pentecost? Why does it tell us about the feeding of the five thousand, and why does it record the leaders of the Jerusalem church telling Paul, 'See . . . how many thousands of Jews have believed' (Acts 21:20)?

Of course, numbers are not everything, but numbers are an important indicator of growth. I cannot understand how leaders who have had fifty people in their church for ten years can think that's OK or even acceptable to God. Thank God for the fifty people, but we are not here to hold the fort. We are here to advance the kingdom. The church is not a hospital, but an army with a medical corps. We should provide help for wounded soldiers, but tending the wounded is not the primary task of an army. It is difficult to be a large church in the British culture. There are few role models to inspire, and a mindset which says that only small is beautiful. Margaret Thatcher (not often quoted in books of this kind!) referred to the nation's inherent distrust of anything larger or more successful than the average as 'the tall poppy syndrome'. Excellence and a desire to reach for the exceptional is perceived as a threat and cut down rather than honoured. This cultural trait has seeped into the church as well. Extreme tallness excites curiosity in a way that normal stature does not; it is always noticeable, and therefore causes comment and conjecture. Growth beyond the norm, whether natural or spiritual, intrigues people. Any church larger than a certain size attracts attention and opinions. Many see it as a challenge to their own status quo and therefore wish to discredit it. Others have valid reservations, while still others do not trust anything which is not traditional, British and 'the way we do things here'.

Empire-building?

The accusing cry of 'empire-building' is often aimed at leaders of large churches. The truth is that a self-promoting, empire-building attitude can be present in any organisation of any size. I have met egocentric megalomaniacs with twenty people in their church and no apparent empire, and pastors of churches of ten thousand who are some of the most humble, selfless people I have ever met. Power-hungry people are to be found in every walk of life, proving the point yet again that it has nothing to do with the size of an organisation and everything to do with the human heart. In fact, the only reason people think that this is the exclusive problem of leaders of large churches is because they are the ones who receive the most publicity when something goes wrong. People like Jimmy Swaggart and Jim Bakker would have received no publicity whatsoever if they had been leaders of a small, unknown church, yet their sin would essentially have been no different to God. I am not in any way trying to excuse anyone's sin; I am merely pointing out that our tendency to assume the worst of any successful, highly prominent church leader has no foundation in reality. The little guys sin and fall just like the big guys do – the only difference is that the little guys get no publicity. And the vast majority of leaders of large churches live lives of the utmost integrity and never fall at all.

Empire-building is a heart attitude which is wrong wherever it shows up. Leaders of large churches need our prayers and our support, not our criticism. We need to send a vitally important and urgent signal to such leaders, especially here in Britain. Our message needs to be: 'We are with you, we believe in what you are doing, we need you to keep going, our country needs you and, what's more, the church in our country desperately needs you.'

There is a paradox in the thinking of the majority of Christians in this country which needs to be addressed. They know that God wants the church to grow; they sincerely want more people to become Christians and be added to the church; but they do not like big churches. They feel that when a church becomes large, it loses its 'family feel', it becomes more impersonal, it is too structured and 'professional'. They prefer the church to be small and friendly. But they also agree that large churches have a much greater impact on society, are richer in resources of finance, personnel and talent and can therefore be more effective in evangelism and social involvement. They are simultaneously excited and dismayed when their church begins to increase in numbers. It has to be possible to resolve such a paradox, so that the positive aspects from both angles can be utilised to build the church more effectively.

Superficial worries

It is inaccurate to say that large churches tend to be superficial in relationships or weak in care and sense of family. I have been in enough small churches where these things are also lacking to establish that shallowness or a lack of a sense of family are nothing to do with the size of the church and everything to do with the people in that church. The comment that a large church has lots of peripheral people and that the number of actual, committed church members is far less than the publicised size of the church is also open to challenge. The same ratio of varying degrees of commitment to size of congregation is as much present in a church of fifty as in a church of five hundred or five thousand; it is merely the numerical results which are different.

There is nothing shallow about my home church, nor will there be while we remain clear and committed about the kind of church we believe God has called us to build. As they grow, many churches become confused and shapeless because they do not have a proper definition of the kind of church being built. Everyone in our church knows what kind of church we are building, because we are constantly spelling it out. Everyone has a printed copy of a statement called *The Church I See*, inspired by Brian Houston's similar statement about Hills Church, Australia. It reads like this:

> *The Church I See* is exciting and full of life. It's a church that's both numerically large and spiritually deep.
>
> *The Church I See* is non-religious, naturally supernatural and incredibly fun to be in. It is a church of

renowned character and integrity, a church whose number one priority is to glorify God and bring his wonderful life to a lost world.

The Church I See is attractive, confident, victorious and overcoming. I see a church whose powerful proclamation and awesome worship are broadcast to the nations by every means possible.

The Church I See equips, enables and releases ordinary people to live extraordinary lives.

The Church I See is a deeply committed, loving, caring family, among whom the lonely and the broken find new hope and belonging.

The purpose of this beautiful church is simply expressed for us by the word REED, from Revelation 11:1. Here, the apostle John was handed a reed and told to go and measure the house of God with it. REED has become our acronym for what we believe is the measure of our church's success.

Reach the lost
Establish the house
Equip the saints
Disciple the nations

Everything that we are doing and planning to do must be achieving one or more of these four things. We see people saved weekly, lives turned around and established daily, people equipped, empowered and sent out continually. There is a commitment, vision and love which certainly does not speak of shallowness or confusion.

Membership or partnership?

Some time ago now, we dropped the word 'membership' from our church vocabulary and replaced it with the word 'partnership'. Partnership is a much more dynamic word and concept than membership. People see membership as something to be attained, the goal of any church membership classes we may ask them to attend. Membership for many becomes an end in itself and once you're 'in', that's it. Partnership, on the other hand, is something organic and functional. A person becomes a partner the moment they begin to invest their lives in any way into your vision and mission.

In every church there are members who are not partners and partners who are not members. The writer of Proverbs says, 'A large population is a king's glory, but without subjects a prince is ruined' (Proverbs 14:28). In other words, large numbers are futile unless the people are also partners. Growing churches foster active partnership, not static membership. They invest time, teaching and support, provide opportunities for involved partners and avoid wasting precious resources on maintaining dormant membership. These simple but profound principles are some of those that make the essential difference between small or large churches. The issue isn't how many are members, but how many are involved.

Jesus never said, 'Come and join me.' He said, 'Come and follow me.' The 'passenger mentality' found in many churches springs from the belief that church is something you join. It is not. *'Join' is the language of membership; 'follow' is the language of purpose and partnership*. The word 'membership', to most people in our Western culture, equates with that of the video club or the AA emergency breakdown service. Sadly, many people transfer this thinking to their church life, which then becomes a totally need-centred experience.

For people both to remain and to grow in a large church, two basic things need to happen. First, they need to identify with a small group, and second, they need a job. The small group fosters a sense of belonging, and a job creates a sense of involvement and ownership of the overall vision.

Small groups

Small groups are vital to help people plug into a larger church. It is a sociological fact that people need small groups in order to find a sense of belonging. Many lonely people who have felt isolated and alienated have been greatly helped by the wide variety of small interest groups now available in our local communities. When I first joined my home church twenty-five years ago, it was the existence of small groups that held me and my family in there. We lived in another town miles away, had no transport, no telephone, and were beginning to feel a little cut off. The provision of a small mid-week group in a home closer to us was a Godsend. It was great to get to know people in our group, so that when we came on Sundays there were familiar faces to which we gravitated. To a very large degree, the small group became part of the glue that stuck us into the larger church family. Our group did lots of things together and at times everyone pitched in on decorating, gardening, baking and even house removal. Our sense of community did not come from the larger church but from our small group. Over the past twenty-five years, we have always had small groups in some shape or form, and as leaders we remain totally committed to their unique worth.

I cannot say, hand on heart, that every homegroup meeting was a blessing. Some of them were a struggle, but this was usually when the homegroup leader tried to turn it into a mini Sunday morning meeting, and to be something that he wasn't.

Small groups need to be relevant, full of life and fun to be in. In other words, the overall ethos of the church must be present in each constituent part. These groups should not attempt to be a small-scale Sunday morning, nor should they be allowed to decide their own agendas. In my local church, we have prescribed what each group does on each night they meet. This is not in any way to try and stifle 'grass roots' initiative, but rather to release people and leaders alike from the pressure of wondering what to do each time they meet. The monthly schedule runs to a pattern of an informal breaking of bread together the first week, with friendship night the second week. This is where everyone is released from homegroup to do things with non-Christian friends, neighbours or community groups. On the third week the groups gather for prayer, and on the fourth week there is some kind of teaching of the word, conducted in an informal, chatty style, with lots of opportunity for question and answer.

The benefit of this structure is several-fold. First, there is the removal of pressure from the homegroup leader. Second, a healthy combination of breaking bread, evangelism, prayer and teaching on a monthly cycle is promoted. Third, this structure lends itself comfortably to the development of new leaders, because it hands them a week-by-week proven formula that they just have to flow with and facilitate. Fourth, the whole church is breaking bread, in prayer and studying the word at the same time, albeit in over fifty different locations.

It is important to keep these groups to a manageable size. We try not to allow our groups to grow to more than twenty people. We have found that this is probably the optimum number; beyond it, the group is in danger of becoming too impersonal. This obviously means that there must be a constant encouraging of new leadership, not waiting until the groups are bursting at the seams but well in advance. We must have a pro-active policy of training and empowering people by giving them more responsibility, so that things don't become 'pot-bound', with restricted roots limiting people's growth.

One of the reasons we are slow to bring new people through into leadership is that we are too particular and set the bar of qualification too high, so that few if any can get over it. Yet if the bar had been set as high when the present leaders were at the beginning, most of them would not be in leadership today. I am not advocating that we put unsuitable people into leadership, but I do believe with all my heart that much of the help we need is already present: often we simply fail to see it, because we are looking at too narrow a band of people. Take a look at the motley crew around Jesus. These twelve young men were a ragtag bunch from varying backgrounds, who couldn't even get on between themselves. The extremes of an impetuous Peter, an over-cautious Thomas and a warped

Judas Iscariot leave hope for us all. Yet these were the ones whom the Father chose for Jesus to pour his life into, and between them they went on to write history and change the world for ever. These men spoke with such courage and authority that in Acts 4:13 the Sanhedrin were astonished when they 'realised that they were unschooled, ordinary men'. Do you have any unschooled or ordinary men or women in your church? God sees them as potential world shakers, and so should we!

Getting a job

When it comes to giving people a job, we believe in the deeply theological principle of just getting stuck in! We discourage people from specialising too early on, and find that they eventually gravitate to their preferred areas of ministry by doing what needs to be done, rather than by waiting for their speciality to be identified.

We also run a NICHE programme, inspired partly by a similar programme at Saddleback Community Church called SHAPE. NICHE stands for

Natural abilities
Imparted gifts
Character
Heart
Experience

This programme exists both to help people find the areas they most feel suited to and to show them just how many areas there are. It's a kind of spiritual 'job club'. Every three months, we specifically invite all the new church partners who have been added to us to come along on two consecutive nights to a NICHE programme. The first night is where we describe what NICHE is all about and help people to identify their own natural abilities, heart leanings and experiences. At the end of the first night, each person is given a profile sheet to fill in about themselves and asked to return with it on the following evening. On the second night, each person has a one-to-one informal interview with a NICHE guide, who helps them to narrow down their chosen area of service and involvement. Eventually, each department head or ministry leader is informed of people who have shown particular interest in serving in their area, and is asked to contact these new people and make arrangements for them to be involved in their chosen sphere.

We currently have over a hundred different ministries in the church, and if none of these suit people we encourage them to consider creating a new ministry to add to those we already have (for example, our new car maintenance ministry team, which sprang from the desire of some of the mechanics in the church to serve single parents, widows and unemployed people with free car repairs and maintenance). The important thing is that we put people to work as soon as possible, and have a structure to facilitate that.

When most people walk into a church meeting, they see a minority up front doing all the work while the majority sit and passively watch. We must find ways to show people behind the scenes of church life, and open their eyes to the huge amount of work requiring so much time and personnel for a growing church to be built.

Will the true church please stand up!

If we could shout across the nation, 'Will the true church please stand up!' I wonder who would get up? Would it be the thousands of 'goose-bump' Christians, who have become bored with the biblical disciplines of God's word, prayer and discipleship and now travel the country and the world, chasing the latest thing to be hailed as a new move of God? This is surely not the behaviour of the church Christ died for, and it's certainly not the one he plans to come back for!

Or would it be the 'church-hopping' Christians who, like modern-day Jonahs, having had a problem in one place think the answer is to relocate to another? I know people who have moved to the other end of the country and even overseas, thinking that a change of address will solve their problem. Disappointment eventually sets in with the realisation that *the problem is not geo-graphic but 'cardiographic'. Remember, wherever you go, you're there!*

Or would a call for the true church to stand rouse a response from the 'satellite TV' Christians? That is, the growing number who stay at home and have a weekly 'virtual church' experience through their television set rather than gathering with God's people. It has become more convenient to tune in than to turn out.

The truth is that all these groups are AWOL believers at a time when the church needs them most. God has called general quarters across the church, and it's time for all hands on deck. The days of the jumbo-jet church – three hundred passengers and twenty exhausted crew – are over. The church is a battleship, not a luxury liner, and church leaders should not be here to ensure people's comfort, but to disturb it.

It often takes a crisis to bring about an identification of God's true church. The early church had several, not the least of which was the Ananias and Sapphira episode (Acts 5:1–10). Following this shocking incident, the record states that three things occurred. First, great fear seized the whole church. Second, there was a fresh release of the supernatural. Third, no one else dared join them. The awesome fear of God made people think twice about joining a church where you could be carried out feet first if your life wasn't right. However, we also read that while no one else dared join them, God kept adding to their number. *Men join, God adds*. One is of human origin, the other divine. An addition is an incremental increase; it is extra to what was there before in quality as well as quantity. If a crisis occurs within your church, do not be too quick to write it off as a total loss situation. God will use it for his pruning and growing process, to identify those who are truly part of all that you are doing

From the crowd to the core

There is an important distinction between the crowd and the core. This applies to any organisation, but is particularly significant for the church, where our aim is to transfer as many as possible from one to the other. Jesus, on his travels through the Jewish countryside, was himself struck by the lost quality of the crowds he saw wherever he went: 'When he saw the crowds, he had compassion on them, because they were harassed and helpless, like sheep without a shepherd. Then he said to his disciples, "The harvest is plentiful but the workers are few. Ask the Lord of the harvest, therefore, to send out workers into his harvest field"' (Matthew 9:36–8).

Jesus' love was stirred for the crowd because he saw that they were powerless, troubled and confused, with no way of escaping from their condition. He likened them to sheep without a shepherd – lost, wandering, vulnerable to predators, timid, directionless, fearful and without ownership. His longing was to change all that and bring them to the Good Shepherd. The crowd is not an existence that God wants us to be part of. It is an entity from which he wants to draw his people, and to which he then sends them to bring out more, into the core of his kingdom. The dictionary defines a crowd as 'a mass, mob, populace of spectators, any group photographed but taking no part, background incidentals. A faceless, nameless, numberless body of people.' In contrast, it defines the core as 'the heart, centre, essence, gist, kernel of something'.

Christianity is about leaving the lost crowd and becoming God's core, the church. The crowd has no commitment, and without commitment nothing of significance ever happens in life. This is a general principle, not just applicable to the church: personal development, friendships, marriage, employment, education and a relationship with God all require commitment and an acceptance of responsibility. The language of the crowd is of no involvement, no accountability, no duty or ownership. Anything goes, no one rules. Leaving the crowd requires personal commitment, individuality and independent thought.

We must be willing to work with the crowd in order to cull from them the church. We all came from the crowd. *What we must avoid is building a crowd and then calling it the church.* Nowhere in scripture is the picture and language of the crowd used to describe God's church. Instead, the images and descriptions are of relationship, involvement, communication and love; a chosen people, redeemed, called, anointed, a family, a bride, an army. These are terms of belonging and identity, and they are in the plural. The church is you, Jesus and each other in a bond of unity and covenant, with purpose and security.

The church is a family

Many Christians do not understand this and don't see a need to go to church meetings. They do not realise that the church is God's family. Those who do not get involved or remain peripheral treat it, in fact, as if it is another crowd, with little commitment, no responsibility desired, no authority received and no ownership accepted. Such people attend meetings, but do not choose to become part of the family of God in that locality or to put down roots and recognise that they are an integral part of the organic whole. Yet this is not how the Bible depicts church life, nor is it natural in family life. It is when we settle for a crowd and fail to develop the core of the church that the cries of 'shallow' are raised. The numbers might look good, but the essence, the life sap of the church would be shrivelling up, and eventually, the numbers would begin to decline as well.

It is God's desire that every Christian should move

from the fringes of church membership experience and get immersed in the life force of the church family. Of course, being an attender only is fine for a specific time and purpose, perhaps if you have recently moved to the area and you are finding where God wants to place you, or if you have recently become a Christian and are absorbing the culture. It is not a problem if people choose to do that for as long as they need to. But there is loss in staying in the crowd and a huge gain, both individually and corporately, in moving into the core. The church needs *everyone* to do their part in order to function properly. The apostle Paul made this point many times, most graphically perhaps in 1 Corinthians 12:

> The way God designed our bodies is a model for understanding our lives together as a church; every part dependent on every other part, the parts we mention and the parts we don't, the parts we see and the parts we don't. If one part hurts, every other part is involved in the hurt, and in the healing. If one part flourishes, every other part enters into the exuberance.
> (1 Corinthians 12:24–6, *Message* Version)

Being a non-involved and non-functional part of the body of Christ is a violation of the true nature of the church. You need the church – and the church needs you. God's idea of 'together' in the church is family together, not crowd together, with involvement in each other's lives, responsibility, accountability, serving and love. We can help each other and not be threatened by others' help and advice in our lives. I have always valued the input of others into my own life, when God has prompted a care and concern for me in someone else, and that person has had the courage and commitment to talk to me about it. I do not see this as interference, but as part of God's developing me and making me more like him. And I would rather be perceived as interfering than keep quiet when I know that God wants to help someone through me. Much damage has been done in the church and in the wider world when people have kept quiet when they knew something was wrong.

It's so important that we all feel responsible for the growth of the church we are part of, having an eye to the peace and the beauty and the joy of the garden of God. We need to weed out seeds of unrest, depression and negativism and sow seeds of peace, joy and harmony. If everyone does this, then it is impossible for the weeds of division and discontent to grow. Everyone needs to be tilling their part of the garden. We can plant anything we want, positive or negative, so it is important to know what we want and sow it, ensuring that it is based on the manual. Then the beauty, order, quality and wonder of God will be evident in the church.

I believe that the UK needs many more large churches – churches of thousands – which are centres of influence and excellence. People take note of something too large to ignore. Largeness releases the kind of resources and corporate 'clout' that smallness never could.

Wouldn't it be wonderful if, in every town and city of our land, the biggest buildings were church buildings, and the most prolific buyers of land were growing churches? We, as a church here in Bradford, are currently in the process of building a new 2,000-seater auditorium, offices, seminar rooms and conference facilities on our five-acre site overlooking the city. We moved into our present building on the same site ten years ago. As it seats 800, it is now becoming too small for our present growth and future needs. Recently a BBC Radio Leeds interviewer asked me if I was excited about the new building. My reply was, 'No, I am excited about what the new building will allow us to achieve.' *Growing is about people, not property*, and it is the increasing impact on people's lives that such a facility enables us to have that thrills me so much – and God, too.

Key Points

- 'Join' is the language of membership; 'follow' is the language of purpose and partnership.

- The problem is not geographic but 'cardiographic'. Remember, wherever you go, you're there!

- Men join, God adds.

- What we must avoid is building a crowd and then calling it the church.

- Being a non-involved and non-functional part of the body of Christ is a violation of the true nature of the church.

- Growing is about people, not property.

6

Excellence, the Cinderella of church life

The young people approached the dais, a little nervous and self-conscious but ready to make their contribution to the Sunday service. They began their drama confidently enough, but within a couple of minutes it was obvious that we were not going to be able to see anything of it, for no one had moved the lectern, massive potted plants or microphone stands. Nor could we hear the dialogue, for the young people had not got any amplification, a necessity in this big building. After a few more minutes, about six people simultaneously decided to do something about the problems and rushed forward from all parts of the room, grabbing the same objects in their haste and providing an unwelcome distraction to the drama, which was still struggling gamely on. Then a PA man dashed on to the stage and handed microphones to the actors. The last five minutes went smoothly, but the impact of these well-rehearsed youngsters was lost because of all the 'technical hitches'.

The meeting had not augured well from the beginning. Five minutes before the official start time, there were about half a dozen people in the room. In the next few minutes, about three hundred arrived, jamming the car park, the lobby and the loos, and rushing into the meeting in a fluster of greetings, seat-finding and last-minute duties. The service eventually began about a quarter of an hour late, with people still trickling in for some time after that.

I hoped, with a slightly selfish concern about my own preaching 'slot' later in the proceedings, that nothing else would go wrong after the unfortunate episode with the youth group drama. However, that hope was not to be realised. The next 'item' was a group of singers. As they walked out, they looked terrific: confident, smart, well-prepared and radiant, and I looked forward to hearing them. But I had reckoned without the PA team. I did feel apprehensive when I realised the singers were relying on a backing tape rather than a live band, and I was right to feel so. The singers began, and they were superb, but after only a few bars the backing track stopped abruptly. The singers continued without it, but when it came back on it was ahead of them. They speeded up, got back in time and were singing beautifully when the tape stopped again. When it resumed it was at three times the volume, causing everyone to cover their ears.

I was not in faith about my preaching by this time, but I had a word from God to deliver, so, putting my qualms aside, I began with energy and enthusiasm. After a short while, the microphone began to play up, causing havoc with the flow of my speaking. Out of the corner of my eye, I spotted a PA man literally crawling, commando-style, down a side aisle towards me. I valiantly tried to keep my grip on the sermon, while he continued his progress, crawled up the stairs and started attacking the belt round my trousers. Any minute now, I thought, and they'll fall down. My ministry in the USA will be over before it has really started!

Eventually, I was given a hand-held microphone and all went well until I heard another microphone being tapped vigorously, in an attempt to interrupt me. It was the pastor of the church, looking as if he had something of extreme importance to impart. I didn't think much of his timing, but thought that maybe God had told him something of immediacy. I waited expectantly. 'Oh,' he said, 'I've only just noticed. The children are still here. They should be in their own meeting, but we forgot to send them out. In fact, I've forgotten to arrange any children's ministry at all, so can I have some volunteers, please?' Pandemonium ensued as children and adults got up, climbed over chairs, searched for bags, found some leaders and clattered off. Any impact my words might have had was completely lost, and I cut them short, calling people who were sick to the front for prayer. Then the pastor interrupted again, this time to remind people before they left about the offering, which he had also forgotten earlier. I was in the middle of praying for a lady who seemed very ill when there was a cough by my ear. A steward stood there, holding out a collecting bucket. He had passed it all the way down the prayer line, and was waiting for me and the lady to give our contributions. By this time I was so stunned by the whole proceedings that I meekly gave my offering and departed as soon as I could.

That whole meeting was a sign to me that somebody needs to say something about excellence in the house of

God. The anointing and power of God was curbed and undermined there because of the appalling way the meeting was run. The support elements – the administration and logistics – as well as the casual attitude, failed those who had a burden from God to discharge. Although the ministry, in the form of song, music, drama and preaching, was anointed by God, it was almost completely negated by the inefficiency and mediocrity of the rest of the meeting.

Managing the miracle

'Managing the miracle' is a phrase I heard someone use many years ago to describe our responsibility in handling and managing the miracle of increase in our lives and churches. God is performing a miracle in your town or city: it's the miracle of reaching as many people as possible with his love and life. This massive and awesome responsibility will flounder at the first hurdle unless wisely and pro-actively handled. Jesus was a master at managing the miracle. He understood that the natural and the supernatural work together, that one serves the other. We can see this so clearly in the miracle of the feeding of the five thousand (or, more accurately, ten thousand plus, when you add in women and children). Imagine this heaving mass of humanity spread out without walls or fences to hem them in to a definable space. Jesus, with simple instructions, began to manage the miracle. He told his disciples to instruct the crowd to sit down in groups of fifty. This simple but profound piece of crowd management instantly achieved several things. First, it immobilised everyone. Second, it gave Jesus and his disciples the advantage of being able to see over them. Third, it put the crowd into a posture of expecting to receive something. Fourth, it broke the thousands down into manageable size groupings of fifty. Only after the crowd were stabilised and properly positioned did Jesus move to the next stage of administering the miracle that was in his heart.

Imagine Jesus haphazardly wading into this crowd of thousands of people, trying to grab their attention while handing out bread and fish to any available hand as he went by. God is a God of order. Paul, in writing to the disorderly Corinthian church, says, 'Let all things be done decently and in order' (1 Corinthians 14:40, King James Version). Disorder is indecent, and if you have ever been on the receiving end of someone's disorderly handling of your life, you will no doubt wholeheartedly agree. As you read this chapter, you may think that I am exaggerating the state of some churches, but believe me, some churches are so inefficient that they need no exaggeration whatsoever.

Can we please commit to excellence and the management of our miracle? Songs about 'taking this land for Jesus' when we can't even catch someone falling over in a prayer line are ridiculous. Prophesies about the wealth of the nations coming to us when we can't even handle our own household bills are a nonsense. Preaching about taking the city when we can't even take our own bad attitudes is absurd. And fiery rhetoric about the return of Christ when we can't even return a phone call is somewhat hollow. This chapter is not for the faint-hearted, so let all who dare read on!

God is a God of excellence

God is a God of excellence. He is the source of it, for it is in his very nature. The psalmist recognised this when he cried out 'O LORD our LORD, how excellent is thy name in all the earth' (Psalm 8:1, King James Version). Jesus' life embodied excellence, not only in what he did but in who he was. Daniel, a man who followed God's ways, 'so distinguished himself among the administrators and the satraps by his exceptional qualities [or 'the excellent spirit within him'] that the king planned to set him over the whole kingdom' (Daniel 6:3). It was not his charisma or zeal or technical abilities which commended him to the king, but the excellence within him. *Excellence is not an event or instance, but a way of life, an attitude of heart, an internal value that we must commit to in our personal, family and church life.*

The church generally is famous for being a bit of a shambles. Jokes are often made about jumble sales and roof funds. No one expects the church to excel at anything it does. After all, it's made up of a bunch of amateurs with funny beliefs who bumble through life in dowdy clothes and clapped-out vehicles with fish badges on them. The church is good for a laugh at the way it goes about its business and is not to be taken seriously. But God is not laughing.

If his name is excellent, yet the church is mediocre, then the testimony of the church is in direct violation of God's nature. He has chosen us to be the embodiment of himself in the world, so it is vital that all we are and do should have a standard of excellence in order to glorify him. Also, 'we are ... Christ's ambassadors, as though God were making his appeal through us' (2 Corinthians 5:20). How important, then, that we do not contradict his appeal with ineptitude and a perfunctory attitude. Our presentation, our meeting place, the meetings themselves, our relationships with each other and with visitors, must all shine with excellence. Skimping on detail and cutting corners are not glorifying to God. *Excellence is not the same as opulence and extravagance, though many confuse the concepts*. It is possible to be excellent in all we do in the church without being excessive and profligate with the money entrusted to us.

Excellence is fertile soil for growth, both individually and corporately, and growing churches understand this. If the church does not have a passion for excellence but is content to exist and act in an amateurish, mediocre way, then it will remain small and ineffective. The principles of positive growth will not be able to operate, because the environment for growth is inadequate. Jim Rohn makes the point that 'excellence lies in the opposite direction of the normal pull. To attract attractive people you must be attractive yourself, to attract powerful people you must be powerful, to attract committed people you must become committed. Instead of going to work on them, you must go to work on yourself. If you become, you can attract' (*The Seasons of Life*, Jim Rohn Int., 1981). We want to be attractive, because we want to express the nature of God to those who do not know him.

God is concerned not just with doing things, but with doing things right. This is what got King David into trouble and cost Uzzah his life, during the first attempt to bring the Ark back to Jerusalem. While David's desire to do this was right, the way in which he did it was wrong. He realised his wrong when, in 1 Chronicles 15:13, he said to the Levites, 'It was because you, the Levites, did not bring it up the first time that the LORD our God broke out in anger against us. We did not enquire of him about *how* to do it in *the prescribed way*.' God has a prescribed way of doing many things, and the consequences of doing things any old how do not come more seriously than the above.

Shabby buildings, scruffy Christians, disorganised homes, off-hand ways of treating strangers or guests, delayed responses to calls and correspondence and missed deadlines all symptomise a failure to be living with an excellent spirit, and therefore a failure to represent the Lord to those who don't know him. Tom Peters, a secular writer who has tapped into an understanding of excellence which is way beyond that of the church, writes:

> A passion for excellence means thinking big and starting small. Excellence happens when high purpose and intense practicality meet. Excellence is hanging in there long after others have given up trying. It's refusing to leave it alone until it's right. It means that anything less than the best really bugs you, maybe even keeps you awake at night, thinking of how it could have been done better.

(*A Passion for Excellence*, Tom Peters and Nancy Austin, W. Collins and Son, 1985)

Even 99.9 per cent is not good enough

Excellence forces you to pick sides and live with people's disapproval at your interference and insistence in wanting things to be done better. It means making yourself vulnerable, because many people find a passion for excellence threatening. Danny Cox, in his book *Seize the Day*, points out graphically what a difference being prepared to settle for second best would make to the life of a nation.

> 99.9 per cent is not good enough. If it *was* good enough, then in the USA, every year, 2m tax documents would be lost, 811,000 faulty films would be put in cameras, and 22,000 cheques would be taken from the wrong bank accounts in the next hour. Twelve babies would be given to the wrong parents every day if 99.9 per cent was good enough, and 291 pacemaker operations would be performed incorrectly.
>
> (*Seize the Day*, Danny Cox and John Mower,
> Careers Press, 1994)

These amazing statistics are the consequences of such a small margin of error, and show that falling short of excellence really does matter. The mediocre just isn't acceptable, in any aspect of life, and particularly in church life. 'Good enough' is not good enough.

Britain is riddled with a 'that'll do' attitude. We as the church must not be part of it. Yet some of the worst offenders in hopeless administration, late bill-paying and chaotic life organisation are Christians, and pastors in particular. This shameful situation needs to change. We must not put up with mediocrity and shabbiness in the way we are treated or in the way we treat ourselves and others. We need to insist on excellence everywhere and send a signal that it is of paramount importance. Unlike the USA, where the customer really is always right, we in Britain are made to feel self-conscious and embarrassed for daring to raise the issue if service or goods are defective or not up to a reasonable standard. We must be committed to excellence in everything *we* are involved in, and expect excellence in return.

Millimetres and inches

Excellence is a matter of millimetres and inches, not metres and yards. In sport, a fraction of a second can make the difference between world-wide fame and fortune or obscurity. The digital scoreboard showed that three-tenths of a second was all the French downhill skier Jean-Claude Killy won by. But the following year he earned in excess of $2 million, while the competitor three-tenths of a second behind him earned $30,000 as a ski instructor. You don't have to do much as a church to stand out, because church is an arena where average and below is the norm. The golden rule here is do to others as you would have them do to you. If you want to be kept waiting by people, then keep them waiting. If you don't want your phone calls returned, then don't return any. If you want people to ignore important deadlines, then ignore deadlines yourself. A church leader once left me stranded for five hours after a fifteen-hour flight; later that same year he finished up being stranded himself for nineteen hours at another airport. I couldn't help smiling to myself when I heard this news. We always reap what we sow.

A fraction above the average can make a massive difference, for high quality is not achieved in leaps and bounds but in the little extra we put into everything we do. Learn to go the extra mile. There is no traffic jam on that stretch of road, because everyone exits after the first mile. It is in the small adjustments we make in our own attitudes and in the seemingly trivial touches of church life – the manner of greeting, the kind of literature we produce, even whether visitors are offered hospitality or not. Amazing progress towards excellence can be made by positioning the right person in the right place at the right time.

Correct positioning is a major key to the release of a person's and a church's full potential, just as a diamond is at its most beautiful when it is in its right setting. We need the right people in the right setting, so that we can all shine to our maximum. There is no point in trying to force increase to happen when the management of the church is dysfunctional. The wrong person answering the telephone at the church office could lose more people in a week than could be added to the church in a month. Our receptionist, Emma, is brilliant – she is so good that I ring up just to hear her answer the phone! None of these principles cost a lot, but they can make a huge difference to how we present ourselves and our message to a world which is cynical about the church and its way of doing business.

I can already hear some people saying that this all

sounds like American showiness – what really matters are people's lives. But that's exactly my point. People are the ones on the receiving end of everything we do. The way we look after things is an insight into how we will look after people. Jesus made this connection when he asked, 'If you have not been trustworthy in handling worldly wealth, who will trust you with true riches?' (Luke 16:11).

True riches are people's lives and the eternal truths of God's word, which can change lives for ever. If a dilapidated building does not trouble us, we certainly won't be troubled by a person's dilapidated life. If we would allow a disorderly meeting, we will allow a disorderly life, and so on.

In Chapter 4, I tried to show how things work in combination with each other. The issue of excellence works on exactly the same principle. It is all well and good praying for influential people to be added to your church, people who could share so much resource of talent, motivation and practical assets, but influential people understand and rely upon excellence. Many businessmen and senior company managers who depend on a standard of excellence around them to function would be driven crazy by the shambolic way in which most churches are run. The title of this book is *God's Fingerprint*, and if his unique identifying mark is anything, it is certainly excellence.

Observe the ant

Two men were out golfing one day, neither of them particularly good golfers. Suddenly, one of them hit the ball right down the centre of the fairway, something he had rarely achieved. When he reached his ball, he found that not only was it right in line with the green, it was also resting nicely on top of an anthill. Grasping his golf club excitedly, he swung at this sitter and missed it, killing 5,000 ants in the process. Amazingly, the ball was still sitting on top of what remained of the anthill. Once again he swung his club, missing a second time and killing another 4,998 ants. At this point, only two ants remained alive. One of them turned to the other and said, 'If we want to survive we had better get on the ball.' And, church, if we want to survive we had better get on the ball, too!

It is clear from the book of Proverbs that ants are far more organised than people and have much to teach us. Though they have no apparent commander, they march in straight lines, have the foresight to store food in summer for the coming winter, and are extremely co-ordinated and highly focused in their purpose (Proverbs 6:6–8). What about locusts? Proverbs 30:27 tells us that, though they have no king, they advance together in ranks. Do you know how hard it is to get people to move together in rank? We can't get most of the church even to stand together, never mind advance together. But I for one refuse to be upstaged by an ant or a locust, and so should you.

Sheba's submission

When the Queen of Sheba visited King Solomon, she was overwhelmed by the excellence of his kingly admini- stration – so much so that the King James Version notes that she had 'no more spirit in her' (1 Kings 10:5). This queen was no mediocre person herself. When she came to visit Solomon, she brought with her just a fraction of her own vast wealth as a gift for him, yet we read later on that no one had ever before presented him with such massive wealth. She too had palaces, servants, armies and government officials, but there was something about Solomon's life that left her breathless. Note the combination of things that overwhelmed her; they were far more than just Solomon's wisdom. The excellence of the buildings, the meat of his table, the seating of his officials, the attendance of his servants and their immaculate, beautifully made clothes, the appearance and demeanour of his cupbearers and even the magnifi- cent stairway by which he ascended to the house of God were marvellous to behold. For a queen of Sheba's magnitude to be left breathless by another king's stand- ard of quality and excellence was in itself amazing. We are told she came to test him with hard questions, but instead she was overwhelmed, acknowledging that half of it was not told to her.

I believe with all my heart that God wants the world to be left breathless by the excellence of the church. Wouldn't it be wonderful to hear of our visitors, some of whom first come as critics, being left so astonished by what they see and experience that they are reduced to breathlessness by the impact of our corporate excellence?

The WOW! factor

When people come to my home church, they often walk into both our building and our church family and say, 'WOW!' Over the years, we have had the privilege of hosting world-renowned international ministries, top show business celebrities, and major Christian artists, all of whom have said, 'Wow!' about our church family. Even the secular press in our city have said, 'Wow!' about the church, as can be seen in this excerpt from a recent article:

> I went along to a Sunday service to see for myself what is so attractive about this church … Inside the premises on Wapping Road a casual seating area overlooks a breath-taking view of Bradford. I was greeted by about five different people at the door, and even warmly embraced by one woman who I like to think mistook me for someone else. The main hall, which holds more than 800 people, was almost full. Bracing myself for cringe factor ten, I went in. Jasper Carrot once made a dig at the stereotyped, staid Christian, 'looking crap for Jesus'. A quick glance around the hall revealed nothing could be further from the truth about this lot; red nail varnish, swish looking scarves, make up, colour and people of every age. White hair was in the minority, there were teenagers, lads and girls alongside grown men and mums with babies. Loads in their twenties and thirties all chatting as they took their places. The band and choir, all probably under the age of thirty, started up on stage and the sound was loud and highly professional. Cold fish that I am, I

permitted my foot to tap in time with the music, as the people raised their hands in the air in praise. 'I love you, Jesus,' the man was starting to say behind me. 'Let's give applause to the Lord,' said Lara, the worship leader. Unused as I am to this public display, it was not as off-putting as I had dreaded. In fact, I was sorry when the music stopped ... When I looked at the clock it was 1 p.m. yet no one seemed in a rush to leave.

(*Telegraph and Argus*, April 1998)

Having said all the above, no one's 'Wow!' matters if we don't have God's. I believe that God also says, 'Wow!' over our church, and he wants to say it over yours, too. Every church should have the wow! factor – wow! love, wow! friendship, wow! worship, wow! evangelism, wow! music, wow! facilities, wow! leaders, wow! people, wow! administration, wow! receptionist, wow! kids' work, wow! everything! A spirit of excellence will put wow! into your church. Many churches have people who greet at the door, but nobody should greet people like your church does. Our worship is among the most awesome I have found anywhere in the world. God wants the same for your church. When I have the privilege of standing up on Sunday morning and looking across the hundreds of faces in the congregation, I just say to myself – and often to them – 'Wow!' All these wonderful people reflect back at me the amazing grace of God, and sometimes it is so overwhelming I literally feel dazzled and overcome by the brilliance of God's life within them.

There are Glyn and Doris, who some years ago lost their seven-year-old son in a tragic drowning accident, worshipping God with faces like angels. There are Richard and Pat, who two years ago lost their beautiful sixteen-year-old daughter in another tragic accident, their faces aglow with the glory of God as they pour out their 'alabaster box' of extravagant love upon Jesus. There's Gertrude, at eighty-seven our oldest family member, on her feet clapping and swaying to the loud music as if she was a teenager. There are the new converts, saved only a few days ago, just doing what the rest are doing, never knowing that this isn't normal behaviour in church. I look at it all and say, 'O Lord, my Lord, how excellent is your name in all the earth.'

Churches committed to excellence are growing churches, and churches committed to the average and mediocre are either in a holding pattern or already declining. God will not put up with what we put up with; he wants excellence in all we do. Commit today to a spirit of excellence in your life and church. Start now doing whatever you can, however small. Sow excellence into the mix of things. Return that phone call, respond to that letter, be on time and smarten up. Remember, excellence begins with little things and then ends up affecting everything. *Don't look for how to change everything at once; begin with what's right in front of you.*

It is time to bring Cinderella from below stairs and get rid of the two ugly sisters. We are all invited to the King's Ball. It is called the great marriage supper of the Lamb, and I for one am not going to rely on any last-minute magic-wand intervention from the 'fairy godmother'. Some day, our King will come and he will be looking for whoever the glass slipper of excellence fits. It certainly won't fit those two ugly sisters called 'Good enough' and 'That'll do'. Why not make sure it fits your feet? As the Bible says, 'How beautiful are the feet of those who bring good news.'

Key Points

- Excellence is not an event or instance, but a way of life, an attitude of heart, an internal value that we must commit to in our personal, family and church life.

- Excellence is not the same as opulence and extravagance, though many confuse the concepts.

- God is concerned not just with doing things, but with doing things right.

- Excellence happens when high purpose and intense practicality meet.

- Excellence is a matter of millimetres and inches, not metres and yards.

- Don't look for how to change everything at once; begin with what's right in front of you.

7

Does your church have a healthy soul?

God wants us to love him with all our heart, soul, mind and strength, and to do this fully we need to be growing and developing in each of these realms. I believe the issue of a healthy soul is one of the most neglected and overlooked emphases in the body of Christ today. Most churches do not understand the need to develop their soul and are often afraid of even tackling it. The soul encompasses the emotions, will and intellect. However, I want to focus especially on the emotions, affections and passions of our life, because I believe that these are the least developed part of people's soul, especially in the UK. *All growing churches have a healthy soul, because people are drawn to life and life's driving passions and affections spring from the soul.* What you feel most deeply about will shape and become your life, and people will be drawn to that life. Here in the scientific Western world, our reason and intellect have often been over-developed at the expense of our feelings and emotions. Feelings are viewed with suspicion and kept in check by the cultural ethos of our British 'stiff upper lip' mentality. What this has all too often left us with is form without feeling, structure without life, and dead, institutionalised churches. If you want your church to grow, you will have to address this issue of the soul at some point. You may have a great vision, a great plan and great resources, but if there's no life, then there's nothing for people to be drawn to.

Religion has taught us that church is not a place for emotional expression, loudness or exuberance of any kind. Religion has sold faulty counterfeit goods to the public by offering a faith void of feelings, and in doing so has reduced most of the church to a lifeless formality and tradition. 'Feelings cannot be trusted,' cries the cautionary voice of the religious. 'After all we don't want to become "soulish", do we?' *You have a soul and your church has a corporate soul, and that soul does not take care of itself.* Our soul needs to be shown how to love, how to feel, how to obey. Its freedom and wholeness are dependent upon the liberty we allow it to have. If King David had ongoing battles with his soul, we have no reason to think that ours will take care of itself. He was constantly speaking to his soul, instructing it how to respond, demanding its obedience, and calling his feelings and will to come into line with his heart desires. 'My soul will boast in the LORD' (Psalm 34:2); 'Why are you downcast, O my soul? . . . Put your hope in God' (Psalm 42:5); 'Awake, my soul!' (Psalm 57:8); 'Praise the LORD, O my soul' (Psalm 103:1); 'I have stilled and quietened my soul' (Psalm 131:2) and 'He restores my soul' (Psalm 23:3).

There is a massive need in the church today for a restoration of the soul. Sadly, many people had a more liberated soul before they were converted, when letting their hair down at the night-club or football match was a regular weekend event. Yet when these same people come to Christ, they seem to have a personality bypass, and sit in church like wooden Indians with no sign of emotion whatsoever.

Why do you think that the most popular and crowded places in town are the discos, bars and night-clubs? There is more life down at the pub than in most churches, and yet we still wonder why we are not growing. Life is infectious and attractive. People will flock to anything that is bubbling with life. All the growing churches I have ever visited anywhere in the world, though they may differ culturally, socially and historically, have one thing in common – LIFE, and bags of it!

Sadly, religious traditions and legalistic mindsets determine the environment and atmosphere of most churches. Religion is afraid of getting in touch with the real person within. It forbids and restrains the release of a person's soul, for fear that people's emotions will start to spring up in church life.

The prosperity of the soul

John wrote, 'Beloved, I wish above all things that thou mayest prosper and be in health, even as thy soul prospereth' (3 John 2, King James Version). The prosperity of the soul is absolutely vital and takes priority over any other outward expressions of prosperity. The Bible teaches that true prosperity is not in possessions, achievements or riches, but in the condition of the inner world of the soul. Jesus confirmed this truth when he said, 'What good will it be for a man if he gains the whole world, yet forfeits his soul?' (Matthew 16:26).

The richest people in town are not the richest people in town – they are the richest people in soul. The other day I watched a £9 million lottery winner on television who said that he hadn't slept properly for months and was stressed out since he had won the lottery jackpot. Why? Because his external wealth had taken a sudden massive leap, exaggerating the already present gap between his inner and outer prosperity. There is an endless list of people who apparently had it all and yet lived desperate, depraved lives, often dying an early death in some sleazy, drug-related episode. They had tremendous external prosperity and desperate inner poverty.

Some Christians are so stuffy and locked up that they are virtually dysfunctional among any company other than the church. They are afraid to laugh at jokes, afraid to speak up, feel dominated around loud extrovert types, and are generally miserable to have around. As believers, we should have the healthiest and most prosperous soul of anyone, and without that we are living a sub-standard and deficient Christian life. Many of us were raised in an emotionally impoverished environment and as such have never had much soul stimulation, especially in our early years. If Mum and Dad never openly expressed affection to each other, or if your family was more accustomed to stifling their emotions than expressing them, then you may find it difficult to enjoy emotional freedom individually or in the church.

I believe we must commit to developing and stimulating the soul of the church. As I established in

Chapter 2, we can frame whatever kind of world we want, whether our own or the church's. This inner world that we frame will then begin to shape our outer world, this inner heart and soul condition will determine the environment, atmosphere and life of a church family.

In Chapter 6, I described 'The church I see', part of which was 'The church I see is incredibly fun to be in'. Church and fun do not usually go together, but they should. Church should be the place where we have great fun together without feeling bad that we are in danger of being unspiritual and carnal. Don't allow stuffy, religious types to have any strategic involvement in public meetings. The worship leaders, singers, musicians and anyone else involved must be fun people. Even the person giving the notices needs to do it in a relaxed, entertaining way. Those preaching or teaching the word need to enjoy themselves. After all, if the leaders don't enjoy their own ministry, what chance have the people got?

Develop a sense of fun in the church

We sometimes greet each other by giving a shoulder massage. We have thrown our offering in the air, stood on chairs, danced on tables, done the hokey cokey and had spontaneous karaoke. We have had couples waltzing up and down the aisles and conga lines around the room and around the building outside. Some time ago, we had Gloria Gaynor with us in the church. On the Sunday morning prior to her coming, we all sang 'I will survive' in the meeting, just for fun! I could have sworn I saw one or two religious people with their hands raised in worship, thinking it was a church song!

We don't behave religiously on a Sunday morning and then have fun at a separate event. A sense of fun needs to permeate everything you do. We don't just have fun, we are fun! Fun isn't an event, it is you, it is God's church. It sounds strange, but some of us need to learn *how* to have fun, *how* to become a fun person, a person others like having around. Have fun for fun's sake, not as a prelude to the religious bit that some people must tack on to the fun time in an effort to sanctify the whole proceedings.

A sense of fun must begin with the leadership, who all too often walk around looking fed up, as if carrying the cares of the world on their shoulders. If you are unhappy in ministry, you should have the courage to get out of it and find something you enjoy doing. If, as a Christian leader, you are not having the time of your life, then something's wrong. Sadly, many have lost their joy and become inward and closed. They need to learn to laugh at a lot of stuff they are praying about so intensely. Lighten up and get out more! I look at some pastors and think, 'If that's what church does to you, I wouldn't want any part of it.'

'Oh, but brother, there's a lot of pain and suffering in the world,' they might reply. Yes, and there is a lot more joy and freedom in God.

'You see, our church is going through a difficult time.' Difficult times are not half as bad when absorbed into a church with a healthy soul.

Let people with a healthy soul shape the soul of your church

Glenda, my wife is an incredibly fun person. Over the years, she has helped greatly in developing the character and personality of both our natural family and our church family. She has so much flair for anything to do with colour, design, style and layout. Eight years ago, Glenda had the idea of a Christmas cabaret evening. On this evening, we turn our main hall into a cabaret lounge, with huge circular candle-lit tables and waiter service all night. We all invite our non-Christian family and friends, and a combination of secular and Christian music is performed by our own extremely talented musicians and singers. This event has proved so popular with everyone that this past year we had to do two evenings, with over a thousand people in attendance, paying £10 a ticket admission. (The tickets sold out in one hour.)

Every year the number of non-Christian family and friends coming along has increased dramatically. Now the staff of companies where our people work book tickets a year in advance, so that they can come and have their works Christmas party at our Christmas cabaret evening. At the end of the night, we share a simple gospel message, and over the years a large number of people have been born again and added to our church as a result of coming for the first time to our Christmas cabaret. My contribution is usually a rendering of 'Moon River', though this past year I sang a tribute to Frank Sinatra, crooning, 'I've Got You Under My Skin' and 'New York, New York'! Visitors never cease to be amazed that the senior pastor would do such a thing, but they love it.

And importantly, it sets them wondering what the rest of the church must be like if the leader is so lively and entertaining!

I often close such evenings by saying, 'The good news is you have all been to church tonight; the bad news is that you don't realise it.' For people who expect anything to do with church to be dull, boring and irrelevant, these events blow their minds and open them up to some new thinking. People want life; religion is what's left after God's life has gone.

During the year we stage fashion shows, packing the building with hundreds of women and using the catwalk to share Christ with them. Usually one of our models shares her faith and talks about the inner beauty that God brings to a life. A few months ago, we staged an Asian fashion show and had over three hundred Muslim, Sikh and Hindu women in our building having a brilliant time, and at the close of the evening listening to one of our converted Muslim ladies share her faith.

Four times a year, our youth pastor, Steve Gambill, fills the place with hundreds of unsaved young people who come to 'The Rock', a superb music event. God has given him incredible favour in the schools of the city which feed this celebration. The kids can't wait to come, because the whole event is bursting with exuberant life. In between, other events jostle on to the agenda – children's shows, single parents' clubs, hoe-downs, barn dances and karaoke nights – not to mention the Evergreens, our over-sixties, who love to party. Our church is the most fun church I have ever been in – and that is no accident, it is by design. Fun, joy and laughter disarm people and open them up in a way that never ceases to amaze me.

Knowing Jesus is the most fun I have ever had in my life. Of course, we all have difficulties from time to time but, as I mentioned earlier, so do people who win the lottery!

The Alabaster Box Company

Mary of Bethany was an amazing lady. Her story appears in all four gospels, and from them we gain an insight into just how amazing she was (Matthew 26:6–13; Mark 14:1–9; Luke 7:37; John 12:1–8). Of all the places Jesus could have chosen to spend the last few days of his life on earth, he chose the home and company of Lazarus and his two sisters, Mary and Martha. Why not spend these precious last few days in secret retreat with his disciples, saying some final things to them before his crucifixion? Why not spend the time with Nicodemus, or Joseph of Arimathea, two men who could have been of great help to the early church following his departure? Why not spend the time at home surrounded by his own blood relatives? Jesus chose this home because it was the place where he received the greatest acceptance and devotion.

This home was a sanctuary of peace and affection, where Jesus could be strengthened to face the worst hours of his life. Mary's spirit was a great refreshment to Jesus. On the three occasions she is mentioned in scripture, she always finished up at his feet. Mary never preached, performed a miracle or had any public profile whatsoever. Yet this woman's beautiful, worshipful heart and soul must have been a great comfort to Jesus. On the occasion recorded in Mark 14, quite a party had gathered:

Simon the Leper, Lazarus and Martha, who John mentions was serving, the twelve disciples, plus a number of other unnamed guests bringing the total to around twenty to twenty-five people. Suddenly, in the middle of the proceedings something amazing, shocking – and totally unforgettable – happened.

Mary had come to the dinner party with a sealed alabaster stone jar or box. This contained a pint of pure nard, the most expensive perfume money could buy. A pint of this perfume was worth somewhere in the region of £8,000 – a price that makes Chanel No 5 look like dishwater! Nard, or spikenard, which was the name of the plant from which its perfume was extracted, was from northern India and was a favourite perfume among the ruling classes. It was exported in sealed alabaster stone jars to wealthy people across the known world. This perfume was probably Mary's family nest egg. We don't know how they came to own such a valuable object. Maybe it was passed down to them from parents or grandparents. We have no way of knowing whether her brother or sister had any idea that she had brought the alabaster box with her to this banquet in Jesus' honour. What we do know is that her family would feel the financial effects of this costly sacrifice for the rest of their lives.

In one sudden yet pre-meditated act of extravagance, Mary crossed the floor of the room carrying the alabaster box, stood behind Jesus as he sat at the table, broke open the stone jar and poured its entire contents over Jesus' head. I can only imagine the gasps of shock as those watching tried to take in what she was doing. The strong, overpowering fragrance filled the whole house and no doubt the whole neighbourhood. The first to speak were some of the outraged guests who, finding a spokesman in Judas, rebuked her harshly for her extravagant waste. Judas, in a show of false compassion for the poor, immediately pointed out how this perfume could have been put to a better use. Mary, as always, had her attention fastened on Jesus. For her there was no waste. Her most precious earthly treasure was nothing compared to the most priceless treasure of the ages, who was about to be broken for her. Jesus immediately spoke up in her defence. He explained that she was pre-anointing him prior to his burial, something that not even the twelve apostles had realised was about to happen.

Mary had an extravagant heart and soul, which I believe represents normal Christianity. Martha, on the other hand, was always busy, fussing around serving and preparing meals for Jesus that he hadn't even asked for. There are a lot more Marthas than Marys in the church today, and one reason for this is that extravagance towards God is still frowned upon by many as excessive emotionalism. I can still remember, as a young Christian, standing during the worship with tears rolling down my face, overwhelmed by the presence of God. Moments later, two people from the congregation came up to offer to help me with whatever was troubling me. Obviously my emotional freedom was just too much for them, so they had to try and tidy it up. In that church, no one had ever wept in worship before. It wasn't the done thing to express any emotions that might attract undue attention or cause potential public embarrassment. Even though we were a Pentecostal church and thought we were really free, we were in fact locked up in our emotions, and had an impoverished soul as a church.

Mary came to Simon's house with extravagance on her mind. She came determined to do what she did. She had decided that she would not be put off by others who would be present, even though they included the twelve apostles and her own brother and anxious sister Martha. How about you? Do you go to meetings with extravagance on your mind? Do you bring an alabaster box of 'your all' to pour on Jesus? For some (most?) churches the contrary is true. So many come reluctantly, giving average, mediocre and minimal cost responses to him who paid the ultimate price for us. Sometimes I look out across a worshipping congregation and see people who are like sealed alabaster boxes, full of sweetness and fragrance yet too locked up to let it out.

A healthy soul has learnt to be extravagant – bearing in mind that extravagance is an extremely relative term. In one place, lifting hands in worship would be considered extravagant; in another, conga lines around the room would be commonplace. God is an extravagant God, 'in accordance with the riches of [his] grace that he lavished on us' (Ephesians 1:7–8). This verse doesn't say he dabbed it behind our ears or that he dribbled it on us, but 'lavished'. When God gives, it is 'pressed down, shaken together and running over' (Luke 6:38). God's a pourer, not a dabber or a dribbler; he gives extravagantly because he loves us extravagantly and feels deeply about us. If our lives and churches reflect the freedom of soul that Mary displayed, then I believe even a cynical, hardened world will have to sit up and take notice.

Some Bible commentators teach that Jesus was totally alone throughout the last forty-eight hours of his life, but this is not quite true. The fragrance of Mary's alabaster box perfume was with him to the end. When she poured it out over his head it would have gone into his hair, his beard, his scalp and skin. Every time Jesus smelt this fragrance, this aroma of brokenness, he experienced the expression of love which said, 'Jesus, I love you more than my own life, and now, through your brokenness, many millions throughout the ages, just like me, can be reached.' This fragrance was on him as he knelt alone in the agony of Gethsemane. It was on him as he stood before Pilate and as the soldiers taunted and whipped him. This fragrance was on him as they drove the nails into his hands and feet and stood around mocking him at the foot of his cross. I have decided that both I and the church I lead will always be a part of the great global alabaster box company. God is looking for alabaster box churches; extravagant, passionate and fun churches.

Extravagance towards God is not a command, it's a choice. God wants our obedience but would love our extravagance. The church in our country is certainly not known for her extravagance in anything. It is time that we broke open our alabaster boxes of love, devotion and feelings towards him, not just in an emotional moment but as a way of life. It is not without significance that in a room full of men, it took a woman to show the way. A man would have been so intense, analytical and complicated, weighing up the implications and wrestling with the intimidation of the presence of Judas and other key players in the room. The truth is that we don't even remember the others present that day, but we will never forget Mary of Bethany.

Jesus said, 'Love the Lord your God with all your

heart, soul, mind and strength.' Many Christians are not doing this. Instead, they are trying to love God on the cheap by loving him only with their intellect or with minimal emotional gestures. God wants us to love him with all of our being. To try to love God without the emotional part of our soul is like trying to love your spouse without feelings being involved. The fact is that many marriages are lived without emotion, and the autopilot of routine and familiarity takes over and reduces once loving, close couples to no more than lodgers under the same roof.

A healthy soul magnifies God

Mary, Jesus' mother, declared, 'My soul doth magnify the Lord, and my spirit hath rejoiced in God my Saviour' (Luke 1:46–7, King James Version). To magnify a thing means to make it bigger, and our ability as human beings to magnify is a function of the soul. One of the four basic members of the soul is the imagination; the other three are reason, memory and affection. Through the vehicle of the imagination, we have the ability to magnify things. A healthy, prosperous, God-filled soul will only magnify good things. Magnification doesn't make God any bigger, but it makes him bigger to us, and that's good. A church with a prosperous soul enlarges things. It seems to have exaggerated, extravagant responses to situations which others barely notice. Its people worship more passionately, sing more strongly, clap longer and 'amen' the preacher loudly. To the religious outsider, observing, it all appears a little over the top. But God wants his church to be a lot over the top. *A church with a healthy soul is a responsive, exuberant, passionate bunch of people, and God wants that to be your church.*

Four practical tips in developing your soul

Decide to cry when appropriate

Weddings, funerals, a touching story or a weepy film all move us emotionally. Like Jesus, who was in perfect control of his soul, we should be able to express whatever emotion is appropriate at any given time. If anger then anger, if joy then joy, and so on. Jesus even wept tears at the death of his friend Lazarus, knowing that he would soon be raising him from the dead! He empathised fully with the moment.

Listen to music that stirs you emotionally

Personally, I don't listen to much Christian music. I find much of it long on words and short on melody. There are, of course, several outstanding exceptions. The secular music industry has produced some moving and powerful music which stirs the heart and soul – lush mellow strings, majestic brass, R'n'B and soul music. We need to find music, secular or otherwise, that moves and stirs us emotionally, listen to it, enjoy it and learn to flow with it.

Get around people with a healthy soul

Find David's people with panting souls. Find Marys of Bethany. You can spot them easily in meetings. They are focused in worship, cry easily in God's presence, devour the preaching, and don't want to leave when it's all over. You need to be close to people like this and allow something of their freedom to get into you. People with a locked-up soul tend to hang around other people with locked-up souls. We become like the company we keep. Sometimes we need to break away from the impoverished soul crowd and allow ourselves to be shaped by people who are free. Get around people with a healthy sense of humour, not cynical or sarcastic but wholesome. Spend time with people with varied interests and hobbies and refreshing opinions and points of view.

Learn to enjoy simple things

Birds, flowers, trees, stars, mountains, colours, sounds – there is so much to expand the soul and touch the spirit. When was the last time you stood for a few moments admiring a tree or taking in the fragrance of freshly cut grass? A few months ago, Glenda and I stopped our car in the middle of the Arizona desert, turned off the lights, got out and just looked up into the crystal-clear night sky. We had never before seen the Milky Way look so close that it seemed we could touch it. Then, as if it was an especially arranged treat, a shooting star flew across the heavens. It was breathtaking.

Passion

God is passionate and extravagant. Just take a look at him creating the heavens and the earth in Genesis 1 if you don't believe me! Whether we acknowledge it or not, our world is being shaped by passionate people with fired-up souls. Politicians, pop stars and lobby groups of all kinds are moulding our society. Some animal rights activists are so passionate about their cause that they risk their lives for an owl, a tree or a truckload of cattle. These fervent people, whether we agree with their cause or not, have all tapped into a God-given part of their creative being – passion!

To live without passion is only to exist. We were made for far more than existence. Passion is the spice of life. Every marriage was born in passion and every child is the fruit of passion. *Passion will achieve more in a day than a committee can in a year*. While the religious committees of Jesus' day sat discussing his authenticity, the blind were seeing, the deaf were hearing and the dead were being raised. Passionless preaching should be a crime, yet it goes on weekly in churches all across our land. Passionless churches should be shut down, for they continue to model everything badly about the passionate God that we love and serve. The team that plays passionately will win. The musician who plays with passion will excite the soul and the singer who sings with passion will touch people's lives.

'He who wins souls is wise' (Proverbs 11:30)

People are won and influenced towards Christ primarily through their soul, not their spirit. The gospel first touches the emotions and the mind, and then appeals to the will for a decision. I remember years ago a great 'soul winner' telling me, 'First you have to win them to you and then introduce them to Jesus.' The winning of people for Christ does not bypass our lives. We are not incidental to the plot. To win over a person's affections, thoughts and choices towards Christ requires health in our own soul first. Friendship evangelism is all about connecting with the soul in order to bring closure to the spirit. Sadly, many Christians have little or no personality or life with which to win people over. Christians who expect to hit it off with unsaved people do the most effective evangelism. When we have first gained both credibility and authenticity, we can then move to build a relational bridge strong enough to sustain the appeal for a decision about Christ. If unsaved people can't stand the sight of Christians and despise the church, how can we possibly win them? This predicament leads to aggressive adversarial approaches, which do not work. Non-Christians are not evangelistic challenges to be overcome or projects to be worked on, they are living souls to be loved and won.

Healthy souls win souls, and churches with a healthy soul are soul-winning churches.

Key Points

- All growing churches have a healthy soul, because people are drawn to life and life's driving passions and affections spring from the soul.

- You have a soul and your church has a corporate soul, and that soul does not take care of itself.

- The richest people in town are not the richest people in town – they are the richest people in soul.

- Extravagance towards God is not a command, it's a choice.

- A church with a healthy soul is a responsive exuberant, passionate bunch of people, and God wants that to be your church.

- Passion will achieve more in a day than a committee can in a year.

- Healthy souls win souls, and churches with a healthy soul are soul-winning churches.

8

The growth you seek must be in you first

Imagine the job advert: 'Growing church requires growing leaders to match. Present ones have been outgrown.' It could never happen (could it!) but maybe the idea should act as a useful spur to those of us in leadership. Strategy for and encouragement of positive growth in the church, qualitatively as well as numerically, is the primary responsibility, under God, of the leaders. And as with all other aspects of church life, it begins with the individual. Lack of personal growth in a leader affects many lives besides his own, and this creates a unique pressure. The principles of growth already discussed apply to leaders in a particular manner, because of the responsibility they bear and the challenges they face. *For the church to grow, we need to grow growing leaders. The moment a leader ceases to grow, he or she forfeits the right to lead*.

Many churches remain small and ineffective because no one has become deliberate about making them large. There comes a certain point beyond which expansion must be a conscious strategy rather than a natural occurrence. Responsibility for that strategy lies with the leadership. All aspects of growth – the soil, the seeds, the preparation, the timing, the sowing, the fertilising, the nurturing and the weeding – must be considered and acted on. Pastors may say, 'This church isn't growing, we've had the same numbers for years,' but the reality is that something is always growing, even if it's unrest, fear, unbelief or apathy. My contention is simply this: *if a church can grow weeds of gossip, it can grow instead flowers of worship*. If thorns of disquiet are present, then it is possible to replace them with shrubs of peace and joy. Creating and managing such growth is primarily the duty of the leaders. God is not responsible for what grows in our lives and our church – we are. He carefully planted the first garden and then he gave Adam and Eve the task of maintaining it. After a good start, they abdicated, allowing the serpent sin to have access and spoil the beauty. Leaders have a mandate from God to manage the garden they have been given. Where they refuse or neglect to do so, a mixture results which is not the kingdom of God.

The 70 per cent / 30 per cent challenge

Some time ago, as I was praying, God spoke to me very clearly and on quite an unexpected subject. 'You are functioning at 70 per cent of your capacity,' he said. I was actually quite pleased that he put it as high as that, and was about to thank him for such encouragement when I realised that there was more to come. 'I want the other 30 per cent,' God continued, 'and this last bit of you will cost more than all of the other 70 per cent put together.' Despite the warning in the words, I felt stirrings of excitement as I realised that God was moving me and the church on to a new phase.

As time has passed, I have learnt through experience what I felt was the case in theory. The 30 per cent God referred to is not to do with my workload or ministry in the church: it's to do with me as a person. The cost of leading into something beyond the norm, of heading the charge to largeness, means having one's heart and soul taken apart by God. He wants to ensure that whatever is built around us is in godly, safe hands of integrity, commitment and submissiveness. The process is painful yet necessary, like essential surgery, for he has entrusted us with responsibility for others' lives, and that is one of the most precious things God could give. I once heard someone wisely remark that 'the gateway to ruling is protected by many problems'. God puts obstacles in the way of our destiny to ensure we are properly prepared for the job. There are many people who could have been in leadership but are not, because they were not prepared to give that final 30 per cent. The issue is not improved preaching or being a better leader, but the essence of a person; those innermost motives we keep pretending we don't have, those ambitions we say we're free of but God shows us that we're not, our character flaws, fears, integrity and attitudes. Every aspect of our lives, small and large, is examined, tested and changed. Sometimes he uses circumstances, sometimes other people, to achieve his ends. Often we don't think this is God and rebuke the enemy, but the fact that for all our rebuking nothing changes points to it being God working on us, not the enemy. It feels as if we're on the rack and that even the first 1 per cent is costing more than ever before. I have cried out to God, 'It's not fair! Other people seem to get away with attitudes and actions that I can't even think of without being disciplined by you.' And God's reply, gently but firmly, comes back, 'But others haven't set their heart on what you have.'

And the reason for all this internal pruning and re-planting is to ensure that what is taking place inside us, often hidden from everyone else, is enabling us to grow and to lead. It is so that we are ready to handle the responsibility, pain, accusations, misunderstanding, the discouragement, disappointments and grief that come with giving ourselves to one calling for ten or twenty years of our lives, that we might be part of growing something of significance. It is not about ability, creativity, availability, good ideas or charisma, though we might have all of those. So do many other good people, yet they are not leaders. Inner conflicts have brought down many anointed leaders in the past; issues concerning marriage or family or finance, that remained hidden for many years but were revealed under the pressure of leadership. God wants to deal constantly with all these areas, knowing that possible defeat and certain enemy assault will come there, first and foremost.

From the very beginning of my Christian life, I knew that God was calling me to something different, that I had a destiny in him which went far beyond my situation at the time. In my zeal, therefore, I spent every weekend night until the early hours preaching and talking to people on the streets. Meanwhile, at home, my young wife, with our little girl, became increasingly neglected and frustrated. My response to her complaints about my prolonged absences was that she should willingly sacrifice our family life for the Lord. With a change of church came a challenge to this attitude and advice to spend time with my family and build a strong foundation there, to send them the message that I genuinely loved them more than the church or my ministry. I thought that I had achieved this, despite an inner frustration that I was not fulfilling my destiny with all this 'cutting back' of activities. Then the church organised a weekend away for 'zealous' young men with leadership potential. I was not invited. Everyone going was at my age and stage of life, and frankly, I thought that I was far more qualified to go than some of them.

I was devastated and hurt. The weekend itself was torture for me, and hearing about it afterwards made me feel worse. Eventually, I did what I should have done immediately, and poured out my feelings to the Lord. God reminded me about the wise and foolish builders, and told me that my life and destiny would collapse unless I changed the foundation. I thought that it was based on rock, but God showed me that it was based on the sand of my ego: my calling, my ministry, recognition of me and my abilities.

God builds his house in us first, shaping character, denying ego, and then he builds the church. If we are not founded on him, then disaster will eventually occur. God told me to dig down deep and not to stop until he told me to. Five years later, I was still digging, in my marriage, in my family, in relationships, in attitudes. I was not involved in any leadership at all, went on no weekends away and was not asked to be involved in anything. But

I was at peace with the situation. I was truly happy with my wife and family and not anxious about how our destiny would be worked out. We were just trusting and enjoying God together. Then, when I was secure, standing on a rock with my family at one with me, God was ready to move me on, and he did so. Out of the blue, I was asked if I would consider giving up my job and going to Bible College, with a view to working full-time in the church afterwards. The leadership of the church had seen God at work in the invisible, without me ever having to point it out for them! For God to be able to commit to us the precious responsibilities of his purposes, we need to have a strong, deep foundation. We need to be whole and focused on him, delivered from the frantic nervous energy of trying to manipulate life and trying to get recognised.

I know of a man who was about to be given much increased responsibility within his denomination. He had been involved there for about fifteen years, and was already in leadership. Then, just as he was to be set into a role of greater authority, God revealed an issue within his marriage which changed everything. The other leaders felt they had no option but to withdraw him from leadership altogether while it was sorted out. It is vital that those who are key in our strategy for growth are clear with God in all areas of their life, not just the visible ones. It is easy to assume that the leaders are all strong and that therefore we do not need to be attentive to them, but this is a deception. The strong are the ones who have the vision and the initiative to break through into a new dimension, so they are consequently the ones who will have the greatest enemy activity targeted at them, as well as the greatest scrutiny of God.

I thank God for the people who have challenged Glenda and me at various times in our ministry and guided us on, ensuring that our priorities and motives were right. We all need to be accountable, and not just in some token way. Many people who were models in the past, and who seemed to represent what God was saying and doing, are no longer going on with him. They might blame all sorts of external circumstances, but ultimately it is the strength of a person's inner and private life that becomes the 'make or break'. Therefore, it is vital to encourage leaders in these very intimate areas of their lives. We must not give or receive casual answers to important questions. We need to communicate about fundamentals, irrespective of how a person appears on the outside. We all have choices to make, and some of them will ultimately determine our spiritual destiny, and that of the church we lead.

No perks!

One of the big challenges facing leaders of growing churches is that we require 'all' from volunteers. As Bill Hybels puts it, 'the church is utterly altruistic'. He contrasts hiring a bright recruit in a company, offering him all the perks and incentives of commercial business, with what leaders tell prospective church members:

> You're depraved, a degenerate sinner in trouble with Christ, unless you get squared away with God. And that's what we call the good news, the Gospel. We're

going to ask you to commit five or six hours per week to service, with two or three additional hours for training and discipleship. We're going to ask you to join a small group where your character flaws are going to get exposed and chiselled out. We'll invite you to come under the authority of the elders and give a minimum of 10 per cent of your money. Oh yes, and you get no parking place and no reserved seats. There are no special privileges, no voting rights, no vacations, no retirement programme. You will serve till you die, but trust us, God will make it right in the end.

(Bill Hybels, *Leadership Magazine*, Autumn 1996)

This has to be the worst sales pitch ever!

The fact is that people must be motivated internally. We can try as hard as we like as leaders to create interest and enthusiasm, but we have no power or leverage unless there is an internal 'want to' from the people. The church cannot be run like a company, for business has obvious controls and incentives which the church does not. It is tempting to imagine being able to say to people, 'If you miss next Sunday morning, you lose a day's pay,' or 'There will be double time for all attending the evening prayer meeting.' Numbers would double overnight! But such enticements have no basis in reality, because the church never should or could be a commercial activity but is instead a family, compelled from within and empowered from on high.

The growth you seek must be in you first

Growth requires long-term commitment

Choosing to stay where God wants you is a positive thing, releasing celebration, rather than remaining, like the older brother in the story of the prodigal son (Luke 15:11–31), because no other alternative has presented itself. We need to make a commitment to stay long-term if the church is going to break through into larger numbers. It may not look good on one's leadership CV to stay a long time in one setting, but head transplants, the moving on of leaders after a few years, work against growth, as might logically be expected. Every time someone leaves, there is a pattern of regression, as those left adjust to the change and start again with someone else. God shapes us through the people we lead. He uses them to help us develop as much as he uses us to help them progress. We will meet people who will shock us with what they say and do and who leave still doing so, but leaving is not an option for many leaders. God did not even get involved with Gideon's army until the first 22,000 had left; *then* he started to sift the 10,000 who stayed. God's maths are different from ours; he was identifying the 300 most committed men, proving that it's the heart attitudes, not just numbers, that count. The greatest testing is for those who commit to stay, especially in difficult times, but these are also the ones who in every generation have achieved great things for God. If we want to build for permanence, we simply have to stick around long enough to do it.

As the pace of life in the purposes of God speeds up, there is a corresponding increase in demand on leaders, as the front line in God's army. The standard of requirement is greater because of the responsibility given, and we are dealt with more strictly by God. Moses provides a salutary example of this when, frustrated by the complaints and rebellion of the Israelites, he ignored God and struck the rock to release drinking water for them. Only moments before, he had been in the presence of the 'glory of God' and had been told to speak to the rock. This lapse of obedience and outburst of uncontrolled anger cost Moses dear. He was treated more severely, for more was expected of him (Numbers 20:1–13). We must not allow people-pressure nor other agendas and issues to pull us out from our place of peace, faith and anointing, as Moses did. And we must ensure that we don't dishonour God by striking out in difficult times when a quiet word in the secret place would be sufficient. We need to hear God for a course of action and then stay with it, no matter what obstacles come against it. Those who are hypersensitive need to toughen up, for their own sake as well as for their family and the church. Every conflict one is involved in can leave a sediment in the soul, which is compounded in the sensitive. *A tender heart but a thick skin is required*, otherwise we will become wounded and hurt, a host carrier of a virus of pain, with a life and ministry dogged by problems, infecting others with pain and hurt. More than ever, it is vital that we are centred on God in every area of our lives. Only in this way will the growth we seek be in us first.

God-centred leadership

Sometimes, there is a danger that our leadership slips from being God-centred, because who or what we minister 'under' dominates who we are 'before'. The boy Samuel 'ministered *before* the LORD, *under* Eli' (1 Samuel 3:1, my emphases). He loved God, and was before him, by the Ark of the Covenant, but he was under the priest Eli, who had neglected God's ways and who was in his 'usual place'. As leaders, we can be before God, loving him and wanting to serve him, but still be under something or someone who pulls us away from the centre of God's will for us. We may be under stress, pressure or even the doctor. It might well be the people we're leading or power brokers among them. We might be under the trustees or the governing committee of the denomination or church group we're in. It might be discouragement, wrong expectations, the past or traditions which dominate us. *Whether we intend to or not, we serve what we are under, and that will be imparted in our ministry.* Other people can put burdens and expectations on us which pull us out from under God. Then we can no longer be bold and godly in our preaching and actions. We give away what we are carrying, not what we say we're carrying. The deposit we leave with others is from our heart and life and is conveyed by more than words.

Is our ministry, like Eli, in the 'usual place', a place of routine and comfort, which lacks challenge and has become duty without devotion? If we are not Christ-centred at all times then we must deal with the situation immediately, for the church is in desperate need of God-centred leadership. There are several warning signs which indicate a drift away from God-centredness.

Restless when alone with God

If we are under the domination of a negative force in our lives, then this intruder will rob us in every way, especially when alone with God in prayer. I discovered this myself afresh recently, when I had set aside a morning to pray. After about an hour, I realised that my praying was taken up with concerns and problems. The Holy Spirit said, 'Don't come aside to get time with me and then waste it on problems. Instead, be creative, constructive, refreshing your soul.' Needs are legitimate subjects for prayer, but not when they preoccupy us to the point of distraction from our God-centredness.

Some people are restless because they think they are indispensable. They feel that they must be on call all the time, the sort of person that leaves the mobile phone on even when praying or in a meeting. We need to trust God more and not feel that the full weight of advancing his kingdom rests with us. No one is indispensable and we need to stop behaving like 'SuperLeader', flying in to troubleshoot and solve any difficulties in the church. Such an attitude fosters a dangerous culture of dependency on us. Instead, let's send people to God when they have a problem. Otherwise, people take offence when we can't run round after them, instead of focusing on God. We must not live in fear of people's perception of us and our job. If we do, we'll be worn out, and the church will not grow. Time alone with God should

primarily be used for restoration of the soul, encouragement and deep refreshment, rather than problem-
solving.

*The leaders should have the healthiest spirit, soul and mind
in the church.* Theirs should be the healthiest marriages
and families. Examine the core leadership team, rather
than the whole congregation, to learn whether the church
is God-centred. The core team should be one in expressing a God-centredness and wholeheartedness for him.
Do they look happy – or like stowaways on a kamikaze
plane? Do they radiate Christ – or resemble someone on
Crimewatch? Are they smart and confident, passing on
joy, peace and encouragement to those they are responsible for? To achieve this, leaders need to be especially
diligent in protecting their inner self, since they have so
many extra demands on it. Solomon wrote, 'Above all
else, guard your heart, for it is the wellspring of life'
(Proverbs 4:23). Quality time alone with God is the
principal way to nurture the heart, but it is also important
to protect it from anything which might damage or erode
its strength.

I was reminded of this principle some months ago,
when I got into a situation where my heart and Glenda's
were made vulnerable. We went to spend time with a
couple, and almost as soon as we got there I realised that
I had made a mistake in agreeing to come. The couple
were very negative, wallowing in complaints, bad attitudes and pessimistic thoughts. Nothing that we said of
a positive nature was taken on board, but instead was
countered by more damning information which we
didn't need to know. After a short while, we were drained
and discouraged. Realising that we were not getting

through to these people, but that they were having an effect on us, I felt God telling me to get out immediately, and so I cut the visit short. On the way home, I asked Glenda's forgiveness for having allowed her to be exposed to such discouragement. Some may feel that I overreacted completely that evening, but I know that our inner beings were being compromised and that I had to listen to the Lord rather than conventional politeness. I learnt from this experience that we must be extremely careful where and with whom we spend time, so that we don't come away feeling drained and discouraged. This is not to say, of course, that we do not want to give ourselves to those in need, but that is different from making our hearts vulnerable to haemorrhage.

It should not be necessary to spend hours and hours, weeks and months with people entrenched in their problems. Instead, spend one or two sessions with them, get to the root of the difficulties and then leave it to God. Counselling should aim to change the dependency mentality, not cultivate it. The quicker we can encourage people to be independent of counselling and dependent on God, equipping them to solve their own problems and help others with theirs, the better. I'm sure we have all experienced the person who comes to the church really screwed up with problems and keeps us totally occupied for six months, yet at the end of that time we've hardly made a dent in the person's problems, and nothing has progressed in the church. There has been no time left to lead the rest of church and advance the kingdom, and we are worn out. Inadvertently, we have been penalising the majority for the minority. Jesus never did that. We need to be so wise in nurturing the wellspring of life;

otherwise we will burn out. A heart is for life, not just for leadership. We need to guard it well, and not feel selfish in doing so.

Producing without partaking

Another sign that we have ceased to be God-centred is that we can become so busy making things happen that we are too stressed, worried and distracted to take part properly when they do. We might have the most wonderful, God-filled events planned, but we are so concerned with the details of running them that we forget their main purpose and miss their significance. We might be sitting in beautiful worship, and notice that a light is on when it shouldn't be, or that a steward has neglected to notice a visitor hesitating at the back. It's a bit like cooking a wonderful meal for friends and then being so worn out and aware of errors that you can't enjoy it. It is vital that leaders enjoy all that God is doing: the worship, the preaching (including their own!) the ministry, the evangelistic and social events. God delighted in each section of creation as it was completed, relishing it before going on to the next stage, and we need to follow his example and sip the fine wine of God's goodness and blessing rather than gulping it down and missing the beauty and the purpose.

Religious and professional up front

It's amazing how people often change when they are in front of a congregation! Someone with whom you have just been having a normal conversation about television or the weather suddenly adopts a 'religious' pose as he reaches the front of the room, and his tone and mode of speech are transformed. Sentence structures become more complicated, vocabulary is stuck in a time warp and intonation takes on a weighty, authoritative veneer. Until we abandon the need to appear spiritual, we will never be spiritual. It's important to be ourselves, and not to be afraid to be so. Spontaneity can feel risky, but it is a vital part of family life. Recently, we held a banquet in the church for the young people, and after the meal, when the music was playing, Glenda and I, for no other reason than that we felt like it, leapt on to the tables and danced the night away. The young people were at first stunned to see the senior pastor dancing on the tables with such enthusiasm, but they soon joined in with great hilarity and a brilliant evening was had by all! (They want me at all their parties now!)

Neglect of wife and children

As has been said already, leaders should have the healthiest marriages in the church, and if there is neglect there, even for apparently 'spiritual reasons', it shows that priorities are wrong and that the leader has drifted away from being God-centred. Our families need to know that we love them more than we love the church or our ministry. Telling them is not enough; such love has to be demonstrated by being there, spending time with them, communicating about the significant and insignificant alike, showing what importance and value you place on them. This issue has ruined so many leaderships. It behoves us to learn lessons from the past. If we don't, our ministry will flounder in the end, because it is hollow at the centre.

Control freaks

A leader who is not God-centred becomes a control freak. Perhaps out of anxiety that something will go wrong, he starts to police and control all aspects of church life. In reality, it is because he has ceased to trust that God will take care of it all. Such a person imposes lots of rules and regulations to compensate for poor relationship. Good relationship means that people walk within what boundaries there are out of love, rather than fear. If we need to be involved in and control everything that is going on, then the church will not grow positively, because it will have to stay at the size that can be easily controlled. Instead, we need to trust God and let go of total control. More will be said about delegation and plurality of leadership in Chapter 9.

More structural than relational

This mark of drifting away from God-centredness in our leadership is when we're no longer flowing in the life of Christ, but relying on structures and becoming 'fossil-ised'. *Structure exists to facilitate life, not to repress it.* Good structure in the church should be virtually unnoticeable. Relationships must be paramount and spontaneous, not concerned with positioning. We must not become organisational as a substitute for being organic and relational. Like the human body, the structure needs to keep renewing, evolving. The skin and cells we are born with are all replaced many times by the time we are adults. This is all automatic, with no consciousness or action on our part, and so it should be with the church. If we do not evolve structurally, we will plateau and not grow. As leaders, we need to be prepared to change the way we do things in every area of the church and not be held back by tradition or wrong attitudes and reactions. New wineskins are necessary for new wine, and all the prayer, fasting and evangelism will be useless if we do not recognise this. The issue is not with God but with us; he wants growth but will not entrust it to a wineskin which will rip or spill. If people are with us because they are comfortable with the structure of our organisation and meetings, then they are not truly with us, and from time to time we need to touch and disturb the very thing that they are clinging to. The church will grow when people are captured by a vision of God and what he is doing, and will change anything to achieve it.

It is when we are so distracted by the many demands of running a church that we lose our focus on God and feel the burden of being a leader is unbearable. As we turn our focus back on God, keeping our eyes on him, soaking in his love and worshipping him for who he is, the burden will lift but the pressures and challenges will remain. It is just that we will have the resources to deal with them. The position of leader will not of itself bring pressures; these come when we choose to be a leader and disturb the comfortable. It is when we stick our head above the parapet and decide to do something unpopular or something which we know must be done but which others do not agree with. Paul's charge to Timothy applies to us as well: 'Preach the Word; be prepared in season and out of season; correct, rebuke and encourage – with great patience and careful instruction' (2 Timothy 4:2). Yet as we obey these commands, we come against resistance not only from the enemy but from our own congregations, who at times do not take kindly to rebuke, correction or even careful instruction. They prefer to opt only for encouragement, treating the scripture like a multiple-choice text. This inevitably brings its own pressure and challenge. But after every wedding comes a marriage, and after every new leadership appointment comes a similar commitment which needs to be worked at on both sides so that we may rule well, and the church grow to bear much fruit.

Remember, the growth which you seek for your church must be in you first. A church cannot grow beyond its leadership. It is what John Maxwell calls 'the law of the lid' (John Maxwell, *21 Irrefutable Laws of Leadership*, Word, 1999): the fact that as leaders we can act as a lid, holding down the growth that God wants in the church, because of our own limitation and refusal to let go. *Many things in church life will not change until you do*. As leaders, we must constantly go to work on ourselves, because the more we grow, the more growth potential we'll release into our church. Don't be like most church leaders, who are generally lazy and negligent of their own personal development. Invest in yourself, because a lot is riding on you. Here's to the 30 per cent zone!

Key Points

- For the church to grow, we need to grow growing leaders. The moment a leader ceases to grow, he or she forfeits the right to lead.

- If a church can grow weeds of gossip, it can grow instead flowers of worship.

- A tender heart but a thick skin is required.

- Whether we intend to or not, we serve what we are under, and that will be imparted in our ministry.

- The leaders should have the healthiest spirit, soul and mind in the church.

- Structure exists to facilitate life, not to repress it.

- Many things in church life will not change until you do.

9

Let go to grow

'For God so loved the world that he gave his only son' (John 3:16).Here we have the ultimate act of letting go. God the Father let go of his only son to initiate a new beginning for the world. When his time came, Jesus surrendered his life willingly, making clear to Pontius Pilate that he was laying it down – no one was taking it from him (John 19:11). Perhaps the final and most power-ful evidence of letting go was when Jesus cried, 'It is finished,' after which he bowed his head and gave up, or let go of, his spirit (John 19:30). Jesus didn't drop his head, he bowed it. Like someone leaving the stage for the final time, he bowed out and gave up his life.

In a world where everyone is fighting to keep hold of whatever they already have and grab still more, this principle of 'letting go' is not a popular message. *My* rights, *my* recognition, *my* property and *my* life sum up the spirit of the age. Perhaps more than anything else, our refusal to let go of things has given rise to all manner of unnecessary evils, such as division, competitiveness and estrangement.

'Letting go' is a pattern of life. Our refusal to let go breaks that pattern and interrupts a creational rhythm, to which all of us must submit. *When we let go, everybody wins*. In keeping our life we have lost it, and only when we have let go of our life have we truly found it. Consider a world where no one is willing to give up anything for the benefit of another. No woman would yield her body to carry a baby. No teacher would share knowledge to help another. No one would release their money, resources, time or talent. No one would let go of their love, friendship or compassion. No one would go to war for our freedoms and no one would invest anything into the future. *Letting go is the beginning of more life than could ever be possible by keeping hold*. Letting go makes you a bigger person. The more you pour out, the more life can pour in. The first law of increase is that something must die in order that something else may live. The seed must yield up its life in order to release the growth locked up within it. Jesus put it this way: 'Unless a grain of wheat falls to the ground and dies, it remains only a single seed. But if it dies, it produces many seeds' (John 12:24).

Families must let go

A family must let go to grow. As the children get older, Mum and Dad begin to allow them more freedom to live their own lives. Healthy independence is considered to be good and is encouraged, because parents understand that, without this, their children will never grow to become the people they were intended to be. When they get married they leave their father and mother and cleave to each other, thereby starting a whole new unit of growth potential. This is division by design, and its purpose is growth and propagation. It is not perceived as a threat by the parents that their children want to set up another home. They are still family, still have continuing good relationships, which often become even better than before. All of nature and creation is in a continual cycle of letting go. The problem has never really been with the principle, but with the practice of it.

Church leaders must let go to grow

Christian leaders, I am sorry to say, are some of the most controlling, insecure, won't-let-go kind of people I know. All over our country, thousands of believers vote with their feet every year against dominant, restrictive leadership and either join another church or start their own. I am not advocating letting people do what they want or letting go of anything fundamental. What I am appealing for is a willingness to empower and release other people in order to achieve greater growth. As leaders, we must let go in many ways, some of which we don't even realise are needed. Token letting go just won't do, though there is a lot of it about. Letting someone give the notices as an expression of your willingness to open up the pulpit is hardly the cutting edge of empowerment.

Growing lives and churches are constantly letting go of things. For them, letting go has become an absolute necessity in the process of growth. Below is a list of eight things which I believe are essential to letting go. This list is by no means comprehensive but is an attempt to condense a number of ingredients that I have personally discovered to be important in letting go. Please read these ideas with an open heart and then respond honestly to anything you feel God is speaking to you about, either directly from this list or through indirect associations it triggers in your mind. If you want to be really radical, then why not ask another person who knows you well to give you an honest assessment of how you measure up to this list?

Letting go means delegation

Many people in church leadership seem to believe that they are indispensable and therefore must be at everything. Their days and nights are filled with endless meetings about everything and anything in church life, so much so that people could begin to think that it is not only God who is omnipresent. Though I lead a very large and fast-growing church, I seem to be a lot more accessible than most pastors I know with fifty people. They are always out at meetings, hardly ever see their family, are always counselling someone or attending this or that. To grow we must let go of our need to do everything, to be at everything, involved in everything and having the final say on everything.

Clear-sighted, enthusiastic, capable people will not stay with you if you do not delegate. As leaders, we must honour people by our entrusting to them of important things. Delegation is essential to growth, and this doesn't mean letting go with one hand while still controlling it with the other. When I let go of a thing, I let go of it. People around me are often startled by the degree to which I let go and empower and entrust them with what they know is a vital area to me. Now, obviously, we must train people up to a place where we can delegate things to them, but often the problem is not the lack of trained people but the fear of letting go. You say, 'But I won't know what is going on, as I used to.' That's exactly the point; you don't need to know as much as you used to. As you grow, there are more important things that you do need to know, and it is finding out what they are and getting involved in them that will be the key to progress. As a leader, you need to be sure that a system or project is working as it should, with the right motivations and outcomes. Once you see that this is the case, leave it alone! Leaders should then publicly promote and honour those to whom they have successfully delegated. I don't feel embarrassed at all when people in our church ask me a question about a department of the church, and I say, 'I have no idea! You need to ask so and so.'

Remember the leadership-limitation-centred church, mentioned in Chapter 4? Failure to delegate properly anything that really matters sends the wrong signal to good people who want to work with you. What can and should you be letting go of right now? You must let go to grow.

Letting go can mean repositioning

Sometimes letting go may mean stepping aside or stepping down from a role in order to allow someone else better suited to flourish in that function. Much of the church is held to ransom by 'position-minded' people. They have stopped seeing themselves as servants and instead have dug into the bunker of 'position' and office. People doing the wrong job who won't move can stifle growth in a church incredibly quickly. Whatever your role in the church, don't make it your exclusive province. Don't get proprietorial and defensive when anyone suggests some new blood in your department. We must hold all that we have in open hands. That way, there will be no fight to release it when God requires change.

Letting go means forgetting

'Forget the former things; do not dwell on the past. See, I am doing a new thing! Now it springs up; do you not perceive it?' (Isaiah 43:18–19).

Dwelling on the past, whether that past be good or bad, is the enemy of progress. Dwelling on the past affects our spiritual eyesight to the point where we are unable to perceive the new thing that God is doing right in front of us. The Israelites were out of Egypt, but Egypt was not out of them; and this refusal to let go of the past cost a whole generation their lives. Thank God for the past blessings and high points, but we dare not allow a nostalgic, 'good old days' mentality to lay siege to our lives.

The divide between those who dwell on the past and those who don't is often to do with different generations. Those who are older and have been around longer remember how things used to be and can feel threatened by new initiatives and new people. But we must let go of any rearview Christianity: 'Many of the older priests and Levites and family heads, who had seen the former temple, wept aloud when they saw the foundation of this temple being laid, while many others shouted for joy. No one could distinguish the sound of the shouts of joy from the sound of weeping . . . And the sound was heard far away' (Ezra 3:12–13). Did you catch the significance? Those who were older and had seen the former temple wept aloud at the sight of a new beginning. How sad that many older people, leaders included, can be so locked up in the past that instead of being in the forefront, equipping and encouraging the next generation, they are trying desperately to retain control and keep things as they are. It is a sad historical fact that every new move of God has been persecuted by the previous one. People at the vanguard of the last move often inadvertently become the critics of and main resistance to the new thing God is doing. I believe that many who resisted the recent moves of the Holy Spirit could have been some of the most helpful in showing the next generation how to avoid some of the pitfalls that they, by experience, already knew about. It is not enough to criticise someone retrospectively; we need instead to play our part in shaping things as they happen. Anyone can be an expert in hindsight. We need on-the-spot involved consultants, not armchair critics.

I have seen whole churches split over the introduction of an electric guitar or the removal of the pipe organ. I'm not talking here about sixty years ago in some dead traditional church, I am talking about today, in the so-called Spirit-led churches. I know of one Pentecostal church where three people left over the introduction of an overhead projector, because they saw the possible replacement of hymnbooks as a sin against God and a betrayal of their spiritual roots. I know of church leaders who are afraid to introduce the changes they so desperately want because some of the older members refuse to let go. Each Sunday morning, these won't-let-go-to-grow people sit with arms folded, looking stern, like the church Mafia trying to intimidate the leadership. They successfully tamed and contained the last leader and now it is your turn! Remember, in Chapter 1, how I explained that 'containment' can kill you.

The prophet Joel summed up how God desires things when he said, 'Your old men will dream dreams, your young men will see visions' (Joel 2:28). *When the dream of the old and the vision of the young are working in tandem together, watch out, devil!*

Letting go sometimes means letting people go

Some people need to leave us in order for growth to be released. They may, unwittingly, be like Lot to Abraham and have become a hindrance and a blockage to the increase that both they and we seek. Not all leaving is bad. People left Moses, David, Jesus and the apostle Paul, and they will leave you. Until we settle and come to peace about the fact that people will leave us, we are not ready to grow. Don't always see people leaving your church as a negative experience, and, conversely, don't let people who do leave with a bad attitude project that back on to you or the church. Are there some people who you know need to leave you in order to release more growth? Let go to grow.

Letting go means knowing what's important

There are actually very few things which are of fundamental importance to the Christian life. Jesus reduced it all down to two basic things: love God with all that you have got, and love each other in the way you yourself would want to be loved. This leaves us with lots of room for flexibility on the rest. Whether we meet at 10 a.m. or 10.30 a.m. is not of fundamental importance. Whether we have the offering and announcements before the worship or afterwards is not of fundamental importance. You may be thinking, 'Well, of course these things are not fundamental,' but, believe me, to some people they are. When we make the mistake of treating everything as having equal importance, weight and value, we unnecessarily create conflict. Many churches are not growing because they have so many rules and regulations about things that don't really matter.

In the Pentecostal church where I started off in my Christian life, we were riddled with rules – rules about dress code, length of hair, hem-lines, make-up, alcohol, materialism, smoking, television viewing, to name but a few. We were so caught up with legislating for things that hardly mattered that we failed to address the real fundamentals. Immorality, divisiveness and rebellion were in the church, but no one seemed to want to address those issues. The apostle Paul described a whole host of topics that we have a tendency to become extremely legalistic about as 'disputable matters' that we should avoid making judgments on and rules about (Romans 14:1–7). Paul's final appeal, in conclusion, was simply, 'Do not destroy the work of God for the sake of food' (v. 20), and 'Whatever you believe about these things keep between yourself and God' (v. 22). Let go of what doesn't matter and start concentrating on what really does matter. Growing people and churches do this.

Letting go means learning to listen to others

James said that we should be quick to listen and slow to speak (James 1:19). Jesus warned us to be careful what we hear and how we listen (Luke 8:18). Listening is an art and a skill; to be a good listener is a great strength. Listening to others is not easy, especially for strong leaders who are so used to doing all the speaking. When we can't wait for the other person to finish speaking without blurting out our reply, we are not good listeners. When we sit already forming our next response while they are still speaking, we are showing that what we have to say is more important than anything we need to hear. Letting go to grow means that we must be willing to abandon our pre-set and pre-formed thinking and be open to the further influence of others, to whom we should listen.

Letting go to find your bull's-eye

Letting go can mean leaving the realm I call the 'permissive will of God' and entering the realm I call the 'perfect will of God'. *God's perfect will is what you were created to do and to be. God's permissive will is what he will allow you to do and to be.* Most Christians live in the permissive will of God – that is, they live in what God allows rather than what God intended for them. It was God's perfect will for the Israelites to enter Canaan in a matter of days; it was his permissive will that allowed them to wander for forty years in the wilderness. It was God's perfect will that Israel be ruled by him; it was his permissive will that allowed them to have a king of their own choice. It is God's perfect will that all men be saved; it is his permissive will that allows men to reject him.

The perfect will of God is 'bull's-eye living'. It is living life to the full, in the place of maximum scoring, maximum power, maximum peace, maximum provision and maximum presence. It is time to find our bull's-eye, which may mean letting go of our place or function in the permissive will to move into our perfect centre.

A lot of letting go will be required to achieve this. Not all letting go is necessarily huge repositioning – some of it may be very small but just as vital. Being wrongly placed is to be misplaced, and if we are misplaced we are going to be replaced. If we are misplaced we are occupying someone else's place. Our refusal to let go will not only keep us out of our bull's-eye, but others from theirs. You would be amazed how many other people can be released and how situations can be powerfully transformed by one person's willingness to let go. As you are reading this book, thousands of God's people are literally crossing the globe to be where they should be with whom they should be, to do what they should be doing. Do you need to let go of permissive will living in order to find your bull's-eye? Then begin today.

Letting go means keeping hold of your anointing

In all your letting go, you cannot let go of your anointing or calling. In all our delegating, we cannot delegate or give away our destiny, vision or purpose, or the unique things about us that are part of that. When I speak about letting go, I am not speaking about the things that God gives exclusively to each individual. There is something unique and special that we all bring to life and that we can never give away. There will always be a need for you.

God's carriers

Moses heard the people of every family wailing, each at the entrance to his tent. The LORD became exceedingly angry, and Moses was troubled. He asked the LORD, 'Why have you brought this trouble on your servant? What have I done to displease you that you put the burden of all these people on me? Did I conceive all these people? Did I give them birth? Why do you tell me to carry them in my arms as a nurse carries an infant, to the land you promised on oath to their forefathers? Where can I get meat for all these people? They keep wailing to me, "Give us meat to eat!" I cannot carry all these people by myself; the burden is too heavy for me. If this is how you are going to treat me, put me to death right now – if I have found favour in your eyes – do not let me face my own ruin.'

(Numbers 11:10–15)

This passage of scripture is an amazing insight into the vastness of the leadership burden that Moses felt. The agony of being the target of three million people's complaint and accusation was unbearable. In the midst of this desperate situation, Moses reached an all-time low, and he literally wanted God to take his life. He began to pour out his soul to God, and a slight paraphrase expresses his despairing dilemma like this: ' Why me? What have I done to deserve all this? This wasn't my idea in the first place. I didn't give birth to all these people; they don't belong to me, yet you tell me to carry them all in my arms to the Promised Land, as a mother carries her children. I cannot carry all these people by myself. It's all just too much for me. If this is how it is going to be, I would rather you kill me now than let me face my own ruin.' Here was the essence of Moses' problem. Even though he was surrounded by millions of people, thousands of other leaders and many elders, he felt completely alone in carrying the people. Moses had fellow leaders, but no fellow carriers. No one felt what he felt about the people, no one felt like a nurse carrying infants except him. His life was so bound up with the people's lives that whatever they did deeply affected him. He even felt personally responsible for providing them with food.

Carriers feel very deeply about all sorts of issues, situations and details that others don't even seem to notice. They feel responsible for things that aren't even their responsibility, for they see the bigger picture, not just their part in it. Carrying is a mark of maturity. Everything we carry in life beyond what we need for ourselves is evidence of our concern for others. A child refuses to carry things. Have you ever walked home from school with your children and noticed the gradual transfer of bags, coats and books from them to you? World War III can break out at home when a parent asks a child to move a cup, plate or dirty glass. A child would rather argue about whose cup it is than pick it up, because he just sees a cup. The parent sees untidiness, an accident waiting to happen, a possible stain on the furniture. A mother shopping for the family shops in a very different way to a young single catering for himself alone. She is carrying the burden of everyone's expressed desires and requests as well as the financial restraints upon her. Her decisions are made on the basis of the needs of the whole family, whereas the young single has only himself to consider. Carriers see the bigger picture and sacrifice their own interests and inclinations for the greater good. Moses had an overview of all the people and what was happening in their lives. The leaders among the people saw their small area of responsibility, but Moses could see it all, and it was killing him.

Lifters, shifters and carriers

On a recent trip to New Zealand I sat in the airport lounge waiting for my flight to board. As I looked out of the window, I observed the cargo handler grabbing boxes from the end of the conveyer belt and dropping them on to a waiting truck. What I noticed more than anything else was how briefly he actually handled the boxes. He simply snatched them up, spun around and dropped them. He was lifting and shifting but not carrying them. *Many people in the church are lifting and shifting but not carrying*. God is looking for long-term carriers, not momentary lifters. Carrying requires a greater involvement with the package than simply lifting or shifting. Moses didn't feel he could put down the burden of the people and walk away; he didn't say that he felt as if he was lifting or shifting them, but rather carrying them in his arms into the Promised Land.

Carrying affects your walk

In Kenya, most people walk everywhere and the majority also carry large loads as well – huge packages and bundles which are often completely disproportionate to their body size. They carry these on their heads, shoulders, arms, backs, or strapped round their foreheads and resting on their necks. Others balance their teetering burdens on old bikes or makeshift carts, struggling against the weight to keep it upright. Those carrying burdens walk very differently to those who are not. Many will be bent double or contorted into other uncomfortable positions by the weight, and often they stagger rather than walk. Meanwhile, those without anything to carry quickly overtake, arriving at the destination sooner and with less discomfort. Carrying affects your walk, your posture and your journey. It governs the route you take, the comfort of the journey, your whole appearance. It is not the easy option, but is nonetheless the best choice.

Supernatural heart transplant

God's response to the heart cry of Moses was basically fourfold:
- The help you need is already present.
- It is among your leadership.
- They are already leaders, but not yet carriers.
- Choose seventy of them, and I will take your carrier's spirit and put it on them.

The LORD said to Moses: 'Bring me seventy of Israel's

elders who are known to you as leaders and officials among the people. Make them come to the Tent of Meeting, that they may stand there with you. I will come down and speak with you there, and I will take of the Spirit that is on you and put the Spirit on them. They will help you carry the burden of the people so that you will not have to carry it alone.'

(Numbers 11:16–17)

There are basically two ways to become a carrier: gradually, or suddenly. Even a child improves over time and begins to carry things spontaneously. But with the increased pace that is upon us (see Chapter 10) and the demands of growing a church, we don't have time for the gradual option. As leaders and carriers, we must believe God that what is within us will come upon the people by a supernatural heart transplant, that he might somehow open people's eyes to see what we see and feel what we feel, transforming them into instant fellow-carriers of the load.

As these seventy elders were experiencing a supernatural heart transplant, something fascinating happened. Of all the things that might have happened at this point, prophesying would not have been my guess. I would have expected these seventy elders who now felt what Moses felt to get among the restless people, perhaps, and settle them, or maybe come with ideas about the food crisis. Or maybe some of them might launch a teaching programme to address the murmuring and wailing. But no – the first and most immediate response to sharing in Moses' burden was to prophecy. This is very

instructive, because it demonstrates that *the essential
burden of a carrier is not people's needs but God's purpose.*

Carriers are first and foremost carrying God's
purpose, which for Moses was Canaan, not the people's
demand for meat. As leaders, we must never make the
mistake of serving people's needs instead of God's
purpose. Sadly, for many this is not the case. Leadership
burn-out is widespread and is largely due to carrying
the wrong loads and serving the wrong agendas. Jesus
said, 'Come to me, all you who are weary and burdened, and I will give you rest. Take my yoke upon you
and learn from me' (Matthew 11:28–9). God's idea of
rest is not having no burden, but having the right
burden. His burden is not people's needs but his own
eternal purpose. God is concerned about our needs, but
is not burdened by them.

Eldad and Medad

Of the seventy elders summoned to the Tent of Meeting,
two of them for some reason did not make it. These two
elders were still in the camp amongst the people when
the spirit of Moses came on them. Just like the sixty-eight
at the Tent, they began to prophesy, but unlike the sixty-
eight, whose prophecy caused no stir, theirs did. We can
prophesy all day long at the leaders' meeting and excite
and arouse no one, but when we start saying in the camp
those things that God told us in the Tent, then – and only
then – is progress possible. For some reason the two in
the camp were named while the other sixty-eight remained anonymous. I believe the reason for this was that

their names were so significant and in themselves prophetic that God wanted us to look more closely at them. Eldad means 'God is a friend' and Medad means 'love and affection'. These two expressions more than any other summed up the essence of Moses' heart that they had just received. Moses was God's face-to-face friend, and his love and affection for the people were so intense that his life was bound up with theirs. As leaders, we can achieve anything if we will commit to and work for these two elements to be primary in the camp of our church. Through the dual administration and combination of God's friendship and loving affection, we can move heaven and change earth.

Pillars, not bricks

God is looking for pillars, not just bricks, with which to build and, more importantly, establish his house in the earth. A pillar is a load-bearing column, a carrier. I was visiting a church recently and a man who was a long-standing member was introduced to me as a pillar of the church. He proudly stuck his chest out and extended his hand towards me. I asked him what he did in the church, to which he replied that he was far too busy with his career and para-church activities to get involved in the local church. This man was not a pillar just by virtue of time, for pillars carry weight. Thirty years in the same church does not make you a pillar, but how much weight you are carrying does. Here are six practical expressions of being a carrier.

- Carriers feel a sense of responsibility for the whole work, not just their part of it.
- Carriers attend and support things that don't necessarily involve or require them. They do this simply to show solidarity and encouragement to those who are involved.
- Carriers give financial support above and beyond the level of the average or the norm.
- Carriers deal with things that they see need addressing rather than abdicating because it is not their department. Imagine if an older sister watched her little brother drawing on the lounge walls and did nothing about it on the grounds that it was not her room, so why should she care?
- Carriers are low-maintenance people, strongly rooted in God and responsible for their own walk with God.
- Carriers don't have friendships that would compromise their loyalties to their fellow carriers.

Are you a carrier or just a leader with a badge?

There are many people in churches carrying far more weight than those with leadership recognition. Never promote anyone into leadership who is not already a carrier, otherwise you will have a non-carrying leader, which is a contradiction in terms. If you are the senior leader in your church setting, then ask God to take what's within you and place it upon your fellow leaders and the whole church. Then watch for those who begin to show signs of carrying your heart, and use those people. May

God bless you and surround you with all the carriers you need to achieve the purpose of God that you are pursuing.

Key Points

- When we let go, everybody wins.

- Letting go is the beginning of more life than could ever be possible by keeping hold.

- Dwelling on the past, whether that past be good or bad, is the enemy of progress.

- When the dream of the old and the vision of the young are working in tandem together, watch out, devil!

- God's perfect will is what you are created to do and to be. God's permissive will is what he will allow you to do and be.

- Many people in the church are lifting and shifting but not carrying.

- The essential burden of a carrier is not people's needs but God's purpose.

10

Footmen and horses

God is bringing a change of pace to the church in this generation, a change which necessitates a response from us. I have been reminded recently of God's incredible words to Jeremiah, words which announce this significant change of pace:

If you have raced with men on foot
and they have worn you out,
how can you compete with horses?
If you stumble in safe country,
how will you manage in the thickets by the Jordan?

(Jeremiah 12:5)

God was replying to Jeremiah's heartfelt complaint about how badly things seemed to be going. Jeremiah had been called to be a prophet from his mother's womb. He prophesied from his teens for over fifty years, through the reign of five kings. Throughout this long time, he carried the same prophetic message to a stubborn rebellious Israel – repent or face judgment for your wickedness. Imagine prophesying the same despised message to the same rebellious people for over fifty years! Jeremiah reminds us that we are not just here to bring a prophecy in the meeting, but to bring a prophetic message to our generation. We need a 'long haul' mentality, and have to pace ourselves accordingly.

By the twelfth chapter of the book of Jeremiah, he was probably about fifteen to twenty years into his prophetic ministry. You might think that by this time there would be some positive signs of change and response to his message, if only in a few, but nothing could be further from the truth. Not only was there no repentance, but those against whom he was sent to prophesy were getting worse. They actually seemed to be thriving in their evil, and Jeremiah's words of judgment were being made a mockery. He had also by this time received a number of death threats from his own countrymen, men actually from his own home town (Jeremiah 11:21). The king was beginning to oppose and persecute him, and Jeremiah was being despised and mistreated by all.

Time for a serious word with God

Such dire circumstances meant for Jeremiah – and us too when things keep going wrong – that it was time for a serious word with God. Quarrelling with God is a time-honoured tradition. Moses did it, Job did it and Jonah did it, and perhaps you're doing it right now. But I warn you that quarrelling with God is extremely frustrating, because he is always right. However, all is not lost; the good thing is that *desperation and disgust and an over-whelming urge to shout in frustration at God could mean that you are a lot nearer to your breakthrough than you think.* Look how Jeremiah was utterly despairing when he protested to God,

> I would speak with you about your justice: Why does the way of the wicked prosper? Why do all the faithless live at ease? . . . You are always on their lips but far from their hearts . . . Drag them off like sheep to be butchered! Set them apart for the day of slaughter! How long will the land lie parched and the grass in every field be withered? Because those who live in it are wicked, the animals and birds have perished. Moreover, the people are saying, 'He will not see what happens to us.'
>
> (Jeremiah 12:1–4)

Jeremiah, like others before and after him, poured out his complaint to God, who seemed so unjust as to allow him to be afflicted while the wicked got away scot-free. However, God's response seemed to make the situation worse. The sub-heading in the NIV Bible just before verse 5 is 'God's Answer', yet what follows is not an answer but a question. Don't you just hate it when people answer a question with another question? Car salesmen are experts at it. You ask, 'How much is that car?' and they answer, 'How much do you want to spend?' You ask, 'What will you give me for my car as a trade-in?' and they answer, 'How much do you want for your car?'

Job was a classic example of this principle. For thirty-five chapters he had been pouring out his heart to God, in soul-searching questions for answers to his tragedy. Even his own wife had advised him just to curse God and die, and get out of the hell in which he was living. Eventually, as often happens, three friends of Job arrived and each in turn began to offer their wisdom as to why all this tragedy had come upon him. By the close of the book, Job and his so-called friends had left nothing unquestioned in the search for an answer to his plight. Then suddenly, into this endless litany of questions seeking an explanation for so much devastation in one man's life, the Bible records in Job 38:1 that 'the LORD answered Job'. However, what followed in reply to Job's weeks of questioning was not an answer, but fifty-three more questions so ridiculous that it seemed as if God was playing games with a man on the brink of mental breakdown: 'Who do the lightning bolts report to?'; 'When do mountain goats give birth?'; 'Does the rain have a father?' or 'Who let the wild donkey go free?'

God often appears insensitive to our problems and immune to our questions. What he is doing when he responds in this way is simply showing us that we mere mortals are not even smart enough to know a good day from a bad one, let alone understand everything by our reasoning and clever questioning. He is showing us that because we don't see the bigger picture, we do not understand what is going on. The difference between our perspective and God's is like the difference between having a single piece of a 1,000-piece jigsaw and from it being asked to describe the whole picture, and then seeing the box lid and being asked to do the same. *God has got the box lid of your life. He sees in an instant where everything fits, including even the difficult pieces.*

God does not need time for things to develop before he understands them, but we do. The day Joseph was sold into Egyptian slavery was a bad day. But seven years later, when he was feeding the nations, saving his family and in charge of the whole of Egypt, it was a good day. It can take years for something that happens to you today to develop fully. Some people now are complaining to God, as Jeremiah and Job did, about the dreadful situation they are in. But in a week, a month or a year from now, they will be rejoicing about the very same thing, because only then will they realise it was actually all working together for their good.

God's answer to Jeremiah was uncompromising, jerking him out of self-pity. *If troubles, challenges, pressures and persecutions as slow as footmen can overtake you, what will you do when they take on the feet of horses?* If you're stumbling in safe, flat, open country, what will you do in a thicket? If you are struggling to keep up now, what will you do when God really accelerates the pace? Imagine Jeremiah's shock: he has spent twenty years faithfully serving God, at times in fear for his own life, believing things couldn't possibly get any worse, and now God tells him that it has all been footmen and safe country; from here on in, there is going to be an increased pace – no more the measured stride of the plodding footmen but the swiftness of galloping horses. There will be no more comfort zone of safe open country, but complex, demanding, dangerous, thicket-type conditions. This is the worst possible combination: increased pace with increased pressures, running faster but through a denser, less predictable terrain.

Footmen Christianity

Most Christians and most churches never achieve any-thing great for God, and never leave any significant and lasting mark on this world, because they get so worn out with footmen issues that they have nothing left for the moment that God announces a change of pace. *Footmen issues are the things that thrive in slowness.* The footmen, now known as infantry, are the slowest moving unit of any army. Footmen notice things that others don't, for the simple reason that they have time to. Footmen notice and complain about sore feet, poor rations, bad weather, poor equipment and the officers over them. Sadly, many churches are footmen churches, held in a pattern of moaning about car parking, too many meetings, the building being too hot or too cold, uncomfortable chairs, over-loud music, over-long meetings, the leaders doing a bad job, and a myriad of other criticisms.

I have often felt that we should introduce four excuse-free Sundays a year for all those who are looking for a reason to avoid church. On these Sundays, we should have beds in the foyer for those who say, 'Sunday is my day to lie in.' We should issue steel helmets for those who say, 'If I went to church the roof would fall in.' We should have blankets for those who say it is too cold and fans for those who say it is too hot. We should have hearing aids for those who say he speaks too softly, and ear plugs for those who say he speaks too loudly. We should have calculators for those who like to count the hypocrites who say, 'I can't go to that church, there are too many hypocrites there.' 'No, you come along. There is always room for one more!' Microwave meals would be available for those who say, 'I have no time to make Sunday dinner if I come to church.' Part of the building would be landscaped for those who find God in nature, and finally we should decorate our buildings with both Christmas trees and Easter daffodils for those who have never seen the church at any other time.

The truth is that when you are on the front line, fighting for your life and dodging bullets, you don't care about anything except staying alive. I am afraid that unless many Christians and whole churches alike repent of their petty footmen attitudes, then they won't even hear this announcement of the change of pace, never mind respond to it. Unless we break free from personality clashes, ego trips, grudge-holding, jealousy and fault-finding criticism, then we are doomed to stay footmen churches. In so many ways, we are the answer to our own prayers, and the majority of our containment, about which I spoke in Chapter 1, is of our own making and we must break out to be able to respond. I hear the sound of galloping horses and accelerated purpose, and yet when I look at the church, my heart is heavy. We are killing each other through more 'friendly fire' than any enemy could ever throw at us. It must stop.

Birth without labour

The prophet Isaiah spoke of a spiritual shift of pace by describing it as being like a woman giving birth before she even goes into labour (Isaiah 66:7). 'The days are coming,' recorded Amos, 'when the reaper will be over-taken by the ploughman and the planter by the one treading grapes. New wine will drip from the mountains and flow from all the hills' (Amos 9:13).

What the prophets were saying through these natural analogies was that things would not always be as we have always known them. They announced the coming change of pace and season well in advance, yet all too often to no avail. Many churches have thick files full of similar prophetic words to them; we write songs containing these thoughts, and people like me continue to write books about them, yet little changes. I feel my responsibility is three-fold:

First, to announce what God is requiring me to say without being intimidated by the absence of response or agreement.

Second, to help identify any possible hindrances, and in this book I have tried to identify many.

Third, to labour with all the resources God has given me to make ready both my home church and God's church world-wide for the great end-time revival we all seek.

Here are fifteen predictions that I believe are evidence of this shift of pace, particularly here in the Western church.

1 We will see an increased sense of urgency and boldness to offer closure to the lost (see Chapter 4). As a result, many more people will come to Christ outside of meetings.
2 We will see a restoration of the New Testament emphasis on 'you and your household' being saved, and whole families will come to Christ in a matter of weeks following the first family member's conversion.

3 We will see an increase of powerful, effective and diverse kinds of prayer, with many groups coming together for this.

4 We will see an acceleration of positioning, with people moving in order to be in a position for greater effectiveness and breakthrough. Just a few of these repositionings, especially at leadership level, will bring huge, accelerated changes. We will see leaders who have struggled for years submitting what they are doing to another's greater vision, and by so doing suddenly seeing the growth they always wanted to see but alone could never achieve. I also believe that many small beleaguered churches need to close and throw their lot in with a church with greater vision in their area. It is usually pride more than difference of theology or ideals that prevents this from happening more than it does.

5 We will see churches emerging as places of excellence, which will become major centres for training God's people in how to manage the miracle of increase.

6 We will see the restoration of the role of apostles and prophets. Much of the church is suffering from either apostolic absence or prophetic lone rangers. Apostles and prophets should be harnessed together, the apostle bringing the plan to the people and the prophets bringing the people to the plan.

7 At last we will see massive release of finances into the church, but only to a few people to whom God can entrust them.

8 We will see increased favour and released resources come from influential people in the world towards churches that are influential in their areas.

9 We will see the gap widen between good and

inadequate churches. The gap between religion and life will so widen that even the man in the street will know the difference and be able to speak of it.

10 We will see more churches of thousands emerging, here in the UK, which will become significant in touching the millions in their surrounding areas.

11 We will see a restoration of and demand for a certain kind of preaching. It will be an intensely practical, highly relevant yet powerfully anointed and skilful communication of God's word, leaving people gasping for more instead of wishing the preacher would hurry up and finish.

12 We will see a restoration of the most awesome worship imaginable this side of heaven – worship in which the sick and crippled are healed, captives delivered and the unsaved born again, none of which will require a prayer line.

13 We will see relatively new converts in a seemingly accelerated growth curve carrying surprisingly large responsibility for the length of time they have been Christians, and managing superbly.

14 We will see many attempts at leadership cross-pollination fail. But we will see a handful of God-ordained cross-pollinations emerging, to become formidable forces of advance in our land and beyond.

15 We will see what I can only describe as new hybrid anointings, as the right people team up with the right people. These anointings will develop to become fresh, strong strains of anointing, with powerful immune systems into which satanic forces cannot penetrate. I believe with all my heart that God is bringing together certain combinations of people's giftings, heart and

experiences, the like of which has never yet been seen. These new alliances will become lethal cocktails of anointing which, when let loose, will smash demonic yokes from people's lives and empower them to become spiritual Rambos – the least a match for a hundred, and the greatest a match for a thousand.

Where are God's Bravehearts?

The announcement of a change in pace demands a response, which is best summed up in this appeal: 'Where are God's Bravehearts, and will they come forward?' The film *Braveheart*, starring Mel Gibson, is a true story about a simple man named William Wallace, who one day, from the depth of his soul, said, 'Enough is enough!' and rose up in defiance of British oppression. William Wallace had no idea that he was turning the tide of history, he was just impatient with the whole situation and angry enough to do something about it.

The book of Judges is a book about God's Bravehearts. It is a catalogue of ordinary people who again and again said, 'Enough is enough!' and, unknown to themselves, became a catalyst for a national breakthrough. Judges lists some of the most unlikely people you could ever imagine being involved at all, never mind leading a national revolt. Some of these men were so average and boring, it's as if the writer of the book of Judges couldn't think of anything interesting to say about them. Take the example of Jair, who led Israel for twenty-two years. The record simply says he had thirty sons, who rode thirty donkeys, who ruled over thirty towns, then he died and was buried (Judges 10:3). Or what about Abdon? He had 'forty sons and thirty grandsons who rode on seventy donkeys. He led Israel for eight years. Then Abdon . . . died and was buried' (Judges 12:13). Boring is an understatement! It's like saying, 'Then came Fred who was married to Betty. He drove a Ford and loved fish and chips. Then Fred died and was buried.'

What made these extremely ordinary men become Judges of Israel was a passionate soul that refused to stay quiet. You may say, 'Oh, but I believe it was the anointing of God.' So do I, but anointing without a passion to change things won't achieve anything. *Where are God's Bravehearts as we move into the next millennium? We need them now more than ever*. Where are those who will say, 'Enough is enough!'? We have had enough mediocrity, enough dead religion, enough small-mindedness, enough sin and mixture in the church of God, enough penny-pinching. I was recently speaking at a leadership forum which ended with lunch. I asked my secretary to phone beforehand and inform them that I would be bringing three people with me. They replied that this would be fine providing my friends paid for their own lunch. My secretary asked how much lunch was, thinking that it must be at least £5–10 a head for it to be even mentioned. You can imagine our shock when we were told that lunch was a mere £1 each! If this is what the leadership of the church is like, what chance have the rest got?

Where are those who will say, 'Enough majoring on minors, enough trivia, enough whining, enough of me and my needs'? Where are the Gideons, the Samsons,

Shamgars and Jephthahs? Where are the Braveheart churches doing something outstanding for God in our troubled towns and cities? God is looking for a passionate, Braveheart people who have the cry of freedom in their heart and soul. Every single person reading this book qualifies to join this history-making company. Is your life as ordinary as Jair's or Abdon's? Then you'll do. If your life is as riddled with fears and weakness as Gideon's, then you'll do. Did you get off to a bad start in life, like Jephthah, the son of a prostitute? Then you'll do. Stop waiting to be recognised or called forward, stop waiting for the leaders to sound the charge. God has already sounded the charge, so get up and get fired up. There's a world to be won and a prize to be gained, and it will go to the brave and the passionate.

And finally . . .

It is difficult to know how to end a book about a never-ending truth. Growth and increase are eternal concepts. We will never stop growing and, as Isaiah tells us, neither will God's magnificent kingdom: 'Of the increase of his government and peace there will be no end' (Isaiah 9:7).

As I stated at the outset, I have tried to major on principles and avoid methodologies. Principles are price-less, and I encourage you to take careful note of anything in this book that may be a helpful principle for you or your church setting. *God's fingerprint is not some theory or concept – it is you*. You and I are God's living mark of identification. When people look at our lives and churches, they should be able to see God's hand all over us. Paul wrote to the troubled Corinthian church and reminded them that they were God's letter, God's representatives, his family and shop window to the world. 'You yourselves are our letter, written on our hearts, known and read by everybody . . . written not with ink but with the Spirit of the living God' (2 Corinthians 3:2–3).

God's DNA of increase is in you, and with it you can frame whatever world you choose – a world that will bless not only you but, more importantly, those you were destined to reach throughout your amazing life. You have the strength in God to 'stay strong when it all goes wrong', and you must have the courage to ask, 'Why isn't the growth I seek happening?' Will you believe that 'big is beautiful' and work towards it, and will you commit to bringing the 'Cinderella of excellence' from the basement to the forefront of your life? Remember, the growth you seek must be in you first, and if it is then you will have a healthy and prosperous soul. Finally, we must all let go of something in order to grow, and if we don't then God's accelerated pace of change and advance will pass us by. You are God's Braveheart, created and chosen to make a difference in an oppressed and dying world. You are part of God's heavenly liberation movement, sent on ahead to proclaim freedom to the captives, whoever they may be.

The purpose of this book is to call God's people everywhere out of an 'it could never happen to me' mentality and into an 'it *is* me' mentality. Our lives will be over before we know it, and we don't have another moment to squander on apathy or procrastination. You must begin now to embrace your destiny, which awaits you in Christ.

Get on board the greatest white-knuckle ride of all time, the ride called your life. No one else can live it, only you, so buckle up and scream in anticipation . . . I will see you at the end.

Key Points

- Desperation and disgust and an overwhelming urge to shout in frustration at God could mean that you are a lot nearer to your breakthrough than you think.

- God has got the box lid of your life. He sees in an instant where everything fits, including even the difficult pieces.

- If troubles, challenges, pressures and persecutions as slow as footmen can overtake you, what will you do when they take on the feet of horses?

- Footmen issues are the things that thrive in slowness.

- Where are God's Bravehearts as we move into the next millennium? We need them now more than ever.

- God's fingerprint is not some theory or concept – it is you.

For more information about Paul Scanlon's ministry, or
for a free product catalogue, please contact:

Abundant Life Ministries
Wapping Road
Bradford
West Yorkshire
BD3 9EQ
England

Tel: 01274 307233
Fax: 01274 740698
www.alcentre.force9.co.uk